GOODBYE, WIGAN PIER

GOODBYE, WIGAN PIER

Ted Dakin

ISIS
LARGE PRINT
Oxford

Copyright © Ted Dakin 2008
Illustrations © John Gallagher

First published in Great Britain 2008
by
ISIS Publishing Ltd.

Published in Large Print 2008 by ISIS Publishing Ltd.,
7 Centremead, Osney Mead, Oxford OX2 0ES
by arrangement with
The Author

British Library Cataloguing in Publication Data
Dakin, Ted
    Goodbye, Wigan Pier. – Large print ed.
    (Isis reminiscence series)
    1. Dakin, Ted
    2. Large type books
    3. Wigan (England) – Biography
    I. Title
    942.736082'092

ISBN 978-0-7531-9510-9 (hb)
ISBN 978-0-7531-9511-6 (pb)

Printed and bound in Great Britain by
T. J. International Ltd., Padstow, Cornwall

Contents

A NECESSARY EVIL

Late as usual, I hurried down the centre aisle and squeezed into a front pew. Father Dillon, with his acolytes in tow, climbed the altar steps. The Mass began, and from that moment on I entered into my world of mental ramblings.

This very afternoon I would be acting as a lookout for a gambling school. This was to be my first time. I had been chosen by Fred Pearce, my mate's uncle, and I was nervous but excited.

Father Dillon's stern condemnations filtered through my meditations.

"Money," he said, "can be the root of good as well as evil . . . Money is a necessity of life . . . to be exchanged for food, warmth, clothing and shelter; not to be squandered and misused. He who gambles for gain shall in the end lose everything, his very soul even."

I began to feel guilty. In a short while I would be consorting with the same kind of people our priest was now condemning.

At last the sermon came to an end. Twenty minutes later I was heading pell-mell for home, but calling first on my mate, Ernie Pearce.

Ernie answered my knock: "What's up, Eric?"

"I can't make it this afternoon, mate."

"You what? And after me beggin' Uncle Fred to take thi on. Thanks a lot."

"Summat's come up."

"Oh, aye, an' what's that then?"

"It's personal."

He looked me up and down, and grinned. "Thas bin to church. Thas gone all holy on mi, that's what it is."

"No . . . no . . ."

"Now, now, God might strike thi dead for tellin' lies."

I began to weaken. "Alright, alright, I'll come . . . Now shudup!"

"Good on yer, mate. Don't forget two o'clock on Gambler's Field."

Gambler's Field was a stretch of common land wedged between a railway line, a canal and a high fence at the bottom end of Mayflower Road. With just a narrow gateway in the fence, the place was ideally situated for the business of gambling.

At two o'clock prompt the gamblers arrived. The game began. Ernie jumped on his bike and sped off along the canal towpath which led to Calman's Bone Works.

I took up my position at the fence which gave me an unimpeded view of Mayflower Road. An hour passed. Suddenly, in the distance, I saw the black-clad figure of Father Dillon. I began to panic. I couldn't leave my post, I couldn't hide, and he was heading my way. I tried to think of some excuse for being there. He stopped on the opposite side of the road.

"Is that you, Eric?" He came across. "Looking out for a friend?"

"Er, something like that, Father."

He looked over my shoulder. "What are those men doing, Eric?"

"What men?" I looked back. "Oh, those. I don't know, Father."

He stared intently at the circle of men. "Those men are gambling."

And he began to stride purposefully towards them.

"Bloody hell!" I thought. "I'd better warn them."

I ran past the cleric, and reached the gamblers winded and anxious.

"What's up, lad?" Fred Pearce asked, looking alarmed.

"It's Father Dillon . . . He might cause trouble."

"Take no notice, lad. He's nobody."

The clergyman arrived. "Good afternoon, gentlemen." He smiled. "I bet you're awfully glad I'm not a policeman, hmm?"

"That we are, Father," Fred said with a grin.

"What's the name of this game?"

"Pitch-and-toss, Father . . . Want to join in?"

"Indeed, no, but may I watch?"

I was stunned. Was this the same person who only this morning had condemned the very "evil" that was now in progress? When would the tirade begin? I held my breath.

"You'd better get back on watch," Fred said, giving me a stern look.

4

"Before you go, Eric," Father Dillon said, "I want you to be a witness."

"A witness?"

"Yes, I want you to witness these fine gentlemen making a donation to the church."

"You're gettin' no donation off me," Fred said. "I'm not even a Catholic."

And the rest agreed. No donations!

Father Dillon shrugged his narrow shoulders. "That's a pity really." His voice rose slightly. "For when I call on our most generous Chief Constable for my usual collection, I shall be forced, reluctantly of course, to beg for even more money . . . and I'm sure he'll be asking me why."

"Police know all about our gamblin' schools, that's why every so often they make raids on us."

"But I wonder if parents and teachers know what's going on — young boys consorting with seasoned gamblers. I think not, gentlemen."

"You're threatening us."

"Goodness me, I'm a man of the cloth. I don't threaten."

"Give us a minute," Fred said

The group went into a huddle, and began to converse in subdued tones. Minutes later, Fred broke away and faced his tormentor. "Here you are, Father." He shoved a greasy cloth-cap under the cleric's nose. Who, without a moment's hesitation, produced a drawstring bag, and emptied the contents of the cap into it.

5

"This, my friends, is a truly magnanimous gesture . . . People can be so benevolent and good when the cause is a worthy one."

"Yeah, yeah, you'll 'ave us in tears next."

That particular Sunday saw the beginning of the most unusual church collections I'd ever witnessed. Every Sabbath day the priest would amble across the field, interrupt a game, collect his money, and continue on his rounds.

A month passed. I was at my usual sentinel spot, and Father Dillon was on time. Giving me his same old greeting, he made his way to the ring of gamblers. At the very moment he joined the group I noticed several railway workers dressed in red safety jackets walking along the tracks. Casually, they left the railway line and proceeded down the embankment. I became suspicious. Not one of them carried any tools. Not one crowbar, pick or spade. Shouting, and waving in wild desperation, I ran towards the group.

"The bobbies! The cops! Run for it!"

People began to scatter in all directions. The police, too, began to run, each one keen to capture his man. Father Dillon, confused by the unexpected pandemonium, stood motionless. Breathless with exertion and excitement, I grabbed him by the arm.

"C'mon, Father, run!"

"Run? Me? But why? I'm a priest, I've done nothing wrong."

"The police don't know that . . . They'll swear you're one of us . . . C'mon, run for it!"

"Oh dear."

With the law in hot pursuit and shouting commands of "Stop!" Father Dillon and I ran with a speed which only comes from the fear of capture; but after years of sedentary living, the cleric was soon in trouble.

"Where . . . where . . . are we going?" he panted.

"Trust me, Father," I said, and headed for the canal towpath.

Another hundred yards, and we drew level with Calman's Bone Works. There was no sign of Ernie. Just past the factory Bulrush Pool glinted dully in the afternoon sun. I slowed down, took a grip of clerical cloth, pulled him through a broken fence, and across some patchy grass. The incline between the pool and Calman's was steep and muddy, but a place of refuge.

Even with our wind regained, and the danger now gone, the priest was still apprehensive.

"What shall we do now, Eric?"

"We'll call on Grandad and get cleaned up."

Five minutes later we entered Grandad's terraced house by the back door. The old man, unfazed as usual, laughed out loud.

"Glory be! Saint and sinner ride together. What have you two been up to?"

In the course of getting cleaned up, and sipping tentatively on Grandad's strong tea, I gave him a detailed account of our escapade. After a good belly laugh, he said: "All I can say, you deserve to be caught and branded alike."

"Now just a minute," Father Dillon said. "Ministerial work is part of my vocation. I was there for a purpose."

"What, keeping company with gamblers? You should be ashamed."

"I was collecting for the church . . . I only ran because Eric insisted."

"Then you'd better give this young lad a sincere thank you."

"For treating me like some kind of criminal?"

"For saving you and your church from the stigma of shame; captured, and you'd have been in disgrace like the rest."

"But I'm a priest. Surely that must count for something . . ."

"Not in the eyes of the law. The suit only covers the body; underneath you're like the rest of us, weak and susceptible to temptation . . . Jesus was, why not you?"

"But . . ."

"Own up, man. For a short time you were part of an illegal gambling school; and until the law changes that's how it stands."

"Own up, you say?"

Grandad smiled. "Not to the police . . . Make peace with your God."

Father Dillon was dumbstruck. I'd never seen a man of the cloth looking so sad and bewildered. It was embarrassing.

"C'mon, Father," I said. "Let's get movin'. I think the all-clear's gone."

Once outside, the priest touched my arm. "Thank you, Eric. I can see clearly now what could have been a nasty situation, and I'll be for ever grateful."

A few minutes later, he spoke again. "Your Grandfather's a very persuasive person, isn't he?"

"He talks a lot."

The priest laughed: "Saint and sinner ride together. I like that. Very droll." He paused, deep in thought. "He seems to be a God-fearing man, your Grandfather. Tell me, does he go to church?"

"No, Father . . . He's a bloody atheist."

DO YOU REMEMBER?

Do you remember when every decent, law-abiding person could walk our streets, day or night, in dark or light, without fear? I do.

Now we live in the disturbing times of yobs, happy slappers, muggers and hoodies; all predators, who prey on honest, law-abiding citizens. Times have changed drastically. Daily, we are constantly given details of violent crimes. Muggings, rapes, and murder are on the increase.

And, although shocked and disturbed, we have become somewhat immune. In what was once a better age, violence of any kind was more upsetting. It was discussed, analysed and fretted over in detail. Now, it's taken for granted. Back then the criminal paid the penalty befitting the crime.

Do you remember when there seemed to be bobbies everywhere? I do.

Walking their beats, directing the traffic, directing lost old ladies, and passing the time of day. Now, they are motorised; zooming past in police cars. Today, a pedestrian policeman is a wonder to behold.

It's no wonder criminals have lost their fear of being literally caught red-handed. Yobs, hooligans, louts and burglars seem to be winning. They have no fear. And fear of capture, of being apprehended, was — and still should be — a deterrent.

Gone are the days when you could leave your front door unlocked, bicycles left out and unchained, purses left on sideboards and tables. Not any more.

This was a time of respect. Respect for people and property.

Could it be that — apart from more policing of course — more discipline in the home is the answer to lawlessness?

Discipline and the act of caring went hand in hand. Neighbours cared for the sick and infirm. In times of trouble there were strong, dependable shoulders to lean on. Neighbours gave help to those worse off than themselves; and they didn't expect anything in return either. Not even a thank you. That's how it was in those days.

And do you remember, everyone honoured their Father and their Mother? But if you did wrong, you were disciplined.

Mam was the lawgiver in our house, and ruled with a firm, care-worn hand, which, when the occasion arose, gave a gradely, well-aimed clout across the lug-hole; while Dad, the master of the house, slept soundly by the fire.

And what about discipline in the classroom? Today the liberal thinkers recommend leniency, which has left teachers confused and powerless. But as some of us remember, discipline was part of our schooling; although, it must be said, some teachers sometimes went a mite too far.

Today we have an age of craving. A craving for money, possessions and drugs; and criminals will steal, use violence, and sometimes even kill, to acquire them.

Once, back in another age, in a time that is now just a memory, things were different. Old people were respected and revered. Why? Because they were hard-working, honest and decent folk, who had overcome the trials of poverty and hardship, and were still with us to tell the tale, because, let's face it, old folk and their memories are, without a doubt, the history of life itself.

A TWO-WAY WORLD

Harry Christie lay belly down on a bleak, muddy hillside overlooking a single railway line. He and fifty men or more were about to rob a train.

Jobless and desperate, Harry and his fellow unfortunates were waiting for the colliery engine, which, with several wagons in tow, would soon be steaming to the slag heaps, to deposit, with the detritus of deep mining, shiny nuggets of coal, the very source of heat and profit.

A sheet of freezing rain swept along the valley, bringing with it the eerie wail of the loco's whistle. Harry shivered and thought of his widowed mother. A full grate this coming winter would provide the warmth; this, and cheap but nourishing meals would see them through. A second blast from the oncoming train brought Harry to his feet. Adjusting the sack and coal-hammer strapped to his waist, he set off, sliding, stumbling and cursing, down into the valley below. The driver, ignoring the ragged army of boarders, reduced speed. Harry boarded the nearest wagon. Three more followed him. Almost immediately the train came to a stop. The driver uncoupled the trucks and continued on his circuit back to the mine and a fresh load. After an hour of sorting coal from dirt and stone, Harry's sack was bulging fit to burst. Willing hands lowered it from the wagon onto his broad shoulders.

"Thanks, lads," Harry said.

His journey home took him along the canal. This way back had two advantages. It was shorter by half a mile, and the chances of avoiding Constable Frank Willerby were greatly increased.

As lads, Frank Willerby and Harry had been pals; this was before the Willerby family moved to another area. Frank married, joined the police force and, working hard and diligently in his quest for promotion, returned to his roots. On his return he made more arrests and solved more petty crimes than anyone before him.

Harry, buckling under the weight of his burden, came to his usual stopping place, dumped his sack on the towpath, sat on it and smoked his last Woodbine. Twenty minutes later he was clattering over the cobbles of Mayflower Road.

He appeared from nowhere, or so it seemed to Harry.

"What have we got here, then, Harry? Still in the thieving game, are we?"

"I'm just takin' this washin' round to Mrs. Collins. Why, what's up, Frank?"

Frank Willerby was looking good. Well-built, handsome and well-turned out, he made an impressive figure of authority.

"Still the same old Harry. Very witty, but not very clever."

Harry dropped the sack. "We all can't be brainy."

"Who's the coal for, Harry?"

"Mi Mother. I reckon she's goin' to need it, come winter time."

"I've heard that one before."

"Aye, reckon tha 'as."

"I think you'll be after flogging it, hawking it from door to door."

"Well, if that's what tha thinks, tell damn government give us more dole money."

"We live in a two-way world, Harry. You're either up or you're down."

"I wouldn't be knowin'. I've always been down."

"Anyway, I'm booking you, Harry. In a few days time you'll be getting an official summons, followed by a court appearance."

"Thanks a lot, Frank. Tha a real pal."

"And you can carry the evidence to your backyard. I'll have it picked up later."

"An' thy can bugger off, constable. Carry it thisel."

The following Sunday, Harry was back at the valley, waiting patiently for the coal train. A couple of hours later, with the heat of a late summer sun causing sweat to run copiously, Harry made his usual stop. On this particular day the canal was seething with happy swimmers of all ages, all intent on getting as much enjoyment as possible.

A Woodbine later, Harry made ready for the last leg of his journey. A sharp tug on his coat stayed his actions.

"Mester . . . mester, can you help us . . . ?"

The lad, skinny, white and shivering, was pointing to the still, prone figure of another lad, lying on the canal bank.

"I think he's dead, mester."

Harry elbowed his way through a crowd of onlookers.

"Out the way . . . Out the bloody road!"

The lad was on his back, eyes closed, chest still, his colour waxen.

"Get some help, quick!" Harry ordered.

Harry had once witnessed a policeman giving a youngster artificial respiration and, incredibly, bringing him back to life. Throwing off his coat, he knelt and set to work applying steady but rhythmic pressure and cursing all the while.

"Give it up," someone said. "Can't tha see he's a goner?"

As if in condemnation of this morose observation, the lad gave a stifled splutter, and a choking cough, followed by a spew of canal water. After further spasms, the youngster tried to sit up.

"Take it easy, lad," Harry cautioned.

The sound of an approaching ambulance could now be heard, and shortly, because vehicle access was impossible, two ambulance men came trotting up carrying a stretcher and portable equipment.

The ambulance men, once satisfied with the lad's condition, placed him on the stretcher, and set off for their vehicle, only to be stopped by Constable Willerby, who had just arrived on the scene.

Harry, wary of another confrontation, left his sack on the towpath and hurried towards home. A hundred yards on, he looked back. The policeman, he noticed, was in deep conversation with the boy. Willerby shouted and waved.

"Bugger off!" Harry muttered, and walked on.

Breathing heavily, Frank caught up. "So it was you who saved the lad."

"Aye, an' t'others who pulled him out o' canal."

"That was my son's life you've just saved back there, Harry."

"Eh?"

"Simon came down here without my permission . . . He did wrong and nearly paid with his life."

"Bloody hell, Frank, he's a growin' lad. Tha shouldn't try an' stifle an adventurous nature. He'll end up on his backside if tha does."

"A lad needs to know the meaning of discipline, Harry, otherwise he begins to get big ideas."

"He's thi son, Frank, not a bloody criminal."

"Anyway, thanks again, Harry. I'll be forever in your debt."

Harry cleared his throat: "So tha'll be droppin' them charges, then?"

"That's not possible, Harry. I can't stop the system. Your case has already been processed."

"Thanks a million, Frank. Tha're real gent."

★ ★ ★

Forty-eight hours before his court appearance, Harry had a visitor. His answer to the gentle knocking revealed a well-dressed, handsome-looking woman.

"Harry Christie?"

"That's me, luv. What can I do for thi?"

"My name's Betty Willerby. May I come in?"

"I suppose so, but don't expect much."

She refused his invitation to sit down, preferring to stand near the cluttered dining table.

"I'm here with some good news, Mr Christie."

"That'll be a change."

"Frank has arranged for those charges to be dropped."

"Is he all right? — I mean, he's not had a funny turn, 'as he?"

"It was me who had the funny turn."

"You? How do you mean, lass?"

"It was only by chance that I heard about Simon's accident, and that it was you who saved him."

"Don't worry about it."

"But it was Frank's deceit that got to me. All I heard was a pack of lies and a twisted account of what actually happened."

"That's typical o' Frank, luv."

"Yes, he can be very devious and nasty, can Frank, very nasty."

Harry grinned, "So I've heard."

"Anyway, I'm here with a personal, sincere thank you." She looked around the shabby room. "Can you keep me supplied with coal, Harry? Let's say, £5 worth a week."

19

"By, 'eck, I don't know how much £5 worth o' coal comes to."

"I'll be the judge of that. I'll arrange the collections and payments. The less Frank knows, the better."

She rummaged in her shoulder bag, took out a crisp £5 note and placed it on the table.

"That's an advance on the first order."

"Supposin' that husband o' yours collars me again, what then?"

"You won't be seeing Frank again. Come Monday he's being transferred to another department . . . A desk job, I think."

"And did you 'ave anything to do wi' it, missus?"

"Let's say I know some very influential policemen."

"That figures."

"Well, Harry, it's been a pleasure meeting you, and thanks again for what you did."

"Take your money with you, Mrs. Willerby."

"Pardon?"

"Aye, I may have saved your Simon's life, but that doesn't warrant any reward."

"I didn't mean to offend you, Harry."

"Maybe not, but this isn't just about me saving your son's life. This is about revenge, about you strikin' back at Frank, underhanded, like."

With not another word, Betty picked up the money and opened the door.

"As Frank once said, missus, 'We live in a two-way world.' But I think mine's the better one . . . Don't you?"

He closed the door gently behind her.

DO YOU REMEMBER?

"*Nothing lasts forever*," my Dad used to say, and looking back over the years I now know just how right he was.

In those days of the 1930s, any punishment that was deemed necessary in our household was administered by Mam, while Dad took a back seat. Even so, we all respected Dad's authority, because one look from him had the same devastating effect as a gradely clout from Mam.

But discipline wasn't just confined to family rules and regulations, oh, no. If you did any wrong out on the street, or used cheek to your elders, whoever they were, you were given — and it was expected — a clip around the ear to keep you in line.

But it would happen again, and again, because it was all part of growing up in a society where you took your punishment befitting the wrongdoing.

And isn't it true, Grandparents were always stern and grim, and always lived just a spit away?

My paternal grandparents lived just round the corner from us; and Granddad, a retired canal boatman, spent his retirement on his small allotment behind the house.

If Mam sent me around there on some errand or other, I would be handed a hammer or a spade and get roped in for a couple of hours' hard graft. Excuses weren't accepted. And my reward? Well, some unforgettable advice on how to do a good job and perhaps, just perhaps, a butty smothered with jam or margarine. One or the other, you couldn't have them both. They weren't made o' money you know.

Back then, growing up in times of poverty, possessions, even clothes, amounted to almost nothing. Those were the days when a best suit meant just that, best, and was only worn on Sundays for church, visiting relatives, and for weddings and funerals and christenings.

Things weren't bought because you took a fancy to them; they were bought because they were essential to your needs. Your parents, especially your mam, gave a great deal of thought as to how the family budget was to be allocated.

This was a time before Hoover carpet cleaners, when rugs and mats were thrown over a clothes line in the backyard and attacked with a carpet-beater or stick. When all soap seemed to be carbolic soap. When cleaning agents were at a minimum and only rich folk owned a washing machine. When the flags at your front door were scrubbed clean and your front step gleamed a donkey-stone white, then woe betide anyone who walked on it.

Sunday was our posh day. Best suit and tie, clean shoes, newly baked bread and cakes and pies. Tinned salmon for tea, or plates of Lancashire hotpot with red cabbage. And not forgetting the new multicoloured hearth rug that was saved especially for Sundays, and taken back upstairs on Sunday night to keep it clean and tidy.

22

And why is it you never heard of anyone dying from extreme cold? Because back then the winters were definitely colder than they are today. Snow, ice, frost and fog lasted for days, even weeks; with no central heating, just one coal fire in the living-room and a lavvy somewhere up the backyard, times were tough.

Hot oven shelves for our beds, and two or three brothers to go with them; and positively no thermal underwear. By 'eck wi must have bin tough buggers in them days.

So, when you look around at today's many luxuries, even if you 'aint got much money, you've got to agree wi Dad's quotation: "*Nothing lasts forever.*"

MY DAD WAS A COWBOY

John '07'

I remember it was a Sunday morning and Dad, as usual, was singing a cowboy song. He was always singing them — about cattle drives, gunfights, bank robberies, bar-room brawls, the lot. And all of them true, or so he said.

Dad had a good voice and the lyrics were always catchy and entertaining, and it was this that finally prompted me to ask, "Dad, how is it you know so many of these cowboy songs?"

Dad gave me a steady look, then with a gleam in his eye said, "The only answer I can give you, lad, is that when I lived before I was a cowboy!"

"Lived before? What do you mean, Dad?"

"I died . . . shot probably . . . then I was reincarnated!"

"What's reincarnated?"

"Reincarnation means born again. Rebirth."

"Is everyone born again?"

"There's some who think so."

"Even Mam?"

Dad scratched his chin. "Erm . . ."

Just then, in walked Mam carrying a basket of dirty washing.

"I was just askin' Dad, Mam, did you ever live before?"

"I were just explainin' t'lad about reincarnation," Dad said.

Mam gave him a black look. "There's one thing for sure; if I do come back, I'm coming as a man."

My mind was in turmoil. "But if I lived before, then who was I?"

More daggers from Mam. "I don't know about reincarnation, but I know one thing for sure."

"What's that, Mam?"

"Nine months before you were born, your Dad had a twinkle in his eye; then you turned up."

"I don't understand that, Mam."

"Your dad'll explain, won't you, luv?"

Dad cleared his throat. "I'll tell you one day, lad." I was getting more and more baffled and confused.

Anyroad, one day Dad's conviction that he had been a cowboy became a convincing reality. Jed Coop's pony, Jimmy, had done the rag-and-bone rounds for many years until, one hot summer's day, Jimmy collapsed and Jed had to put him out to grass. However, within weeks, Jimmy collapsed again and never recovered. Jed, hating the thought of retirement, bought a robust sixteen-hand piebald called Patch.

Now Patch had a warm and comfortable stable behind Jed's house, but did his summer grazing on Gambler's Field, which lay at the rear of Calman's Bone Works where Dad was employed.

Every day after doing his rounds, Jed would lead Patch into his stable-yard, unload his cart, give Patch a bucket of fresh water, and remove his saddlery, except for his bridle, by which he led the animal down to

Gambler's Field. However, on this particular day the ritual went drastically wrong.

As horse and master reached the factory gates, the 5 o'clock whistle blew. Patch, startled by the high-pitched blast, snorted and reared causing Jed to lose his grip on the bridle. Patch, now released, set off at a mad gallop, sending several of Dad's colleagues diving for cover. Dad (so the story goes) managed to grab Patch's bridle, then, moving with speed, made an acrobatic leap onto his back, and with a strong pull and soothing words brought the stricken animal skidding to a stop. Then they did a steady canter to a grateful Jed. To the tenants of Mayflower Road, that brave act made Dad a hero and was never forgotten.

And me, well, I was now convinced, irrefutably, that Dad had once been a cowboy.

It's a few years now since Dad went to that prairie in the sky, but every Western film I watch — and I watch a lot — I always think of Dad and Patch, and begin to make comparisons; not with John Wayne, not with Audie Murphy, and definitely not with Hopalong Cassidy. No, Dad was a dead ringer (so to speak) of Randolph Scott — tall, thin-lipped, steely-eyed and ramrod straight. But it's not Scott who I see riding off into the sunset at the end of a picture — it's Dad riding Patch, the rag-and-bone horse. Bless him!

And now that I'm older and wiser, I know what Mam meant when she talked about that twinkle in Dad's eye. You see, when he was thinking about having me, he knew that he would be siring another once-upon-a-time cowboy. Someone he could be proud of. Someone that would carry on the family tradition. It was that that put the twinkle in Dad's eye. Nowt else!

Anyroad, folks, after all this palaver I'm feeling mighty peckish, so I'm about to mosey along to the chuck-wagon, then on to the Silver Dollar Saloon for a bottle of red-eye.

See you on the trail, pardners!

DO YOU REMEMBER?

Do you remember those bygone days when dietitian was just a word in the dictionary? I do. Today it's not just a word. In its plural form it means an army of dietary killjoys, bombarding us with advice on what to eat and what not to eat, and even when to eat it. They tell us what's good for us, what's bad for us, watch our intakes of sugar, salt and fat. Check this. Check that. And on and on it goes.

It's no wonder people are confused and bewildered by this continual attack of dos and don'ts. Even our most basic foodstuff is now viewed with suspicion.

This advisory body of busybodies has taken the pleasure out of eating. They've taken over our lives, and robbed us of our ability to choose for ourselves. They do our thinking for us. But it's not always been like this.

Do you remember the days before the rise . . . and rise of these dietitians? I do.

We, the working classes — the poor folk — even in those penniless times of want, tried to keep a good table. Not necessarily a balanced diet, but a good table all the same.

Good thick broths, made with plenty of vegetables, and left to simmer for ages with a good-sized bone from the butchers, just to give it plenty of goodness, and then mopped up with chunks of Mam's home-made white bread. By 'eck, just the remembering makes me slaver. And what about those home-made steak and kidney puddings which, on slicing open the pastry, let free a flow of meat and rich gravy, that made you dizzy with anticipation? And there were always plenty of spuds. The ubiquitous potato. How can you survive without potatoes? Boiled, chipped, mashed or made into a belly-filling hash. All followed with plenty of rice pudding or Mam's currant cake smothered in butter.

And what about those thick beef-dripping butties! All good body-sustaining food, containing enough stodge — which they now tell us not to eat — to block your arteries just by looking at it. Lovely!

We knew plenty of fat folk, too, and thin; but we didn't make comparisons. There were just fat folk, thin folk, and in-between folk; and that was it.

There were no keep-fit clubs or health clubs or dietitians. We just got on with living, and being ourselves.

Our main exercise was walking. To the shops, work, pictures, pubs and clubs. (Did they have taxi-cabs in those days?) Even our leisure time was spent walking — Haigh Hall, the park, along the canal towpath. If you saw someone running, you knew he'd done something wrong. You didn't run unless you were in trouble.

The cobbler's shop in those days did a roaring trade repairing shoes and clogs. They did a good job, too; thick leather for shoes, and strong irons for clogs.

I remember my Dad, too — to save a few bob — repairing our shoes. The smell of new leather and cobbler's wax, all poignant reminders of a working-class past, will stay with me forever.

DOLLY VARDEN'S
PREDICTIONS

Back in pre-war days, when tea bags were non-existent, when making a brew was a domestic art, Dolly Varden of Mayflower Road ruled majestic. But it wasn't the ritual of the brewing that gave Dolly her prowess — oh no, it was her readings. She read teacups. To be more exact, she read the tea-leaves.

Her clientele, local women with superstitious leanings, swore by her predictions. Jobs, health, marriages and good fortune were all embraced in her visionary forecasts. With two-thirds of the male population unemployed, and their wives desperate for some reassurance that their problems would be resolved, Dolly reigned supreme, and they, the believers, lived in hope.

Dolly's best customer was Betty Bird. Her husband, Tom, was one of the unemployed; but Tom had grown accustomed to his forced indolence. He didn't want work. The very thought gave him palpitations. Anyway, with his dole money, and Betty's pittance for cleaning Doctor Merry's surgery, they could just about manage. He could even afford a few bob for booze and the odd race meeting.

Dolly didn't have a specific timetable for her readings, but Betty always chose Sundays while Tom slept off his midday meal; and this particular Sunday was no different.

Three o'clock prompt, she tapped on Dolly's front door, lifted the latch and entered.

"Are you there, Dolly?"

Dolly, seated at her cluttered dining table, gave her best client a welcoming smile. "I'm always home for you, Betty, dear . . . Take your coat off, sit you down, and I'll stoke up the fire."

Placing an iron kettle on a bed of burning coals, Dolly began her preparations. Space was made for the tea caddy, milk, sugar and teacups.

"Ooh, I'm glad you've come," Dolly said. "I'm gasping for a fag."

Betty, taking the hint, handed over her fee, a ten packet of Woodbines. Dolly, on opening the packet, sniffed, and said, "I'm sorry about this, Betty, luv, but starting next week my fee will have to be twenty, I'm afraid."

"Oh dear."

"I have heard that Maud Pringle charges forty, and her readings are rubbish."

"Who's Maud Pringle?"

Dolly blew smoke. "You don't know her, luv. She lives t'other side o' town." She waved a hand dismissively.

"I've never heard of Maud Pringle . . . What part of town does she come from?"

Dolly coughed. "Ah, the kettle's ready. Shall we make a start?"

A few minutes later, the brewing ritual completed, Dolly threw her fag-end in the fire, and poured two cups.

"Help yourself to milk and sugar, Betty dear." Then, while the hot drinks were cooling, they had a good natter about the latest neighbourhood scandals.

At last, Betty drained her cup, smacked her lips, and placed it gently on the saucer. "That was very good."

Without a word, Dolly took the cup and stared intently into its depths. With a puzzled look she turned the cup anticlockwise, and gazed like some Eastern mystic at the contents.

"Anything?" Betty asked.

"I'm afraid not, Betty, luv . . . Nothing that I can . . . Just a minute." She turned the cup again.

"Does the letter T mean anything?"

"The letter T? I don't think so."

"Wait a minute, there's something else . . . I think it's a bird. Yes, it's definitely a bird perched on the crosspiece of a capital letter T."

"Can I have a look, Dolly?"

"You won't see anything, dear. You have to be blessed with the powers, if you know what I mean. It's taken me years to get where I am."

"Oh . . . If that's it, I'll be off, then."

"Remember what I've told you, Betty. A bird and the letter T. Keep your eyes and ears open, and who knows? Money, even fame could be heading your way."

Deep in thought, Betty hurried home to her husband, who greeted her in his usual foul mood.

"Where's mi flamin' fags?"

Betty took her coat off and began to clear the table.

"That Dolly Varden's got them, 'asn't she?"

"She's got to be paid. It's not much to ask, surely."

"So, you've parted wi' mi last ten fags for one of Dolly's potty predictions, 'ave you?"

"That's right."

"What can we expect this time? Crown jewels, or what?"

"She did well today . . . She got a positive reading."

"Never mind that rubbish! Have you any money?"

That night Tom, flush with the contents of Betty's purse, went to the Three Crowns pub and spent the lot.

It was late the following day when Tom surfaced. Dishevelled and bleary-eyed, he asked for kippers and his newspaper.

"Your paper's come. No kippers!"

"No kippers?"

"No money. Can't buy food without money."

"Uh!"

"There's an egg left. I'll do that for you."

While Betty was busy in the kitchen, Tom was busy, too, studying the day's race meetings.

Betty brought in his breakfast. "We've no money for horses."

"There's one here that's a cert."

"I've heard that before."

"At least I'm tryin' mi best."

"And what do you think I'm doing, eh?"

"You mean goin' round to barmy Dolly's? You've no chance."

"Like I said, she had a positive reading yesterday . . . She saw a bird perched on a capital T."

"A what?" He took a closer look at his paper. "She saw a what?"

"A capital T with a bird resting on the crosspiece. Why?"

"Bloody hell!"

"What's wrong?"

"There's a horse running in the 2:30 at Haydock Park . . . Tommy Robin. By 'eck, it's a 10–1 outsider."

"What about it?"

"What's mi first name, Betty?"

"Tom, of course."

"And the T Dolly saw stands for Tom. What's mi second name, Betty?"

"Bird, you idiot!"

"So there you 'ave it — a robin's a bird, an' Bird's mi name. It all comes together . . . Tommy Robin."

"But your name's Tom, not Tommy."

"Don't nit-pick, Betty. Find us some money, quick!"

"Oh no!"

"Tell mi something, Betty. Has Dolly Varden ever been right?"

"She once told Mrs Sutton her husband would lose a leg."

"But Charlie Sutton's still got his legs."

"Last Christmas Clara Sutton sent Charlie to Fulster's shop . . . You know, the butcher's in't town centre?"

Tom scratched his head. "Aye, I know it."

"Well, he bought a nice leg a' pork for their Christmas dinner, and on't way home he left it in the pub. He never did get that leg back."

Tom had another scratch. "Well . . . there you are. She was right, wasn't she? Are you lendin' mi some money or not?"

Tom got his way, put the fiver Betty gave him on a horse called Tommy Robin that went first past the winning post at 10–1. He was ecstatic; so much so, he gave Betty her five pounds back, plus an extra tenner to buy "some proper grub with". Betty made a silent vow of vengeance.

One Sunday a few weeks later, Tom, now a fully committed gambler, with his winnings dwindling fast, was getting worried. "Goin' to Dolly's today, luv?"

"I am and don't expect any racing predictions, either."

"C'mon, luv, I'm sure you could influence her and make her see summat."

"Stupid bloody man!"

On the way to Dolly Varden's, Betty met Mrs Jones, a complaining old busybody.

"I've just bin tellin' Billy Crispin about the mess those water board men have left."

"What mess?"

"Right in front of mi house — a pile o' dirt, broken flags, everythin'."

"You'll have to complain."

"Don't you worry, I will. Them workmen spend more time leanin' on them spades than diggin' with um."

Once again Dolly's readings came to nothing. On her way home she narrowly avoided a second meeting with Mrs Jones. She was in no mood for another tirade about broken flags, dirt and . . . Wait a minute. Her thoughts raced, her heart thumped. Spades! That was it!

Although Mrs Jones thought otherwise, spades did mean work. She fairly ran the rest of the way. At the front door she paused, took a deep breath and entered.

Tom, disturbed by her entrance, rubbed sleep from his eyes.

"Before you ask, Dolly was fantastic today, Tom."

"Well, what did she see?"

"A spade."

"A spade?"

"And a pick."

"What does it mean, Betty?"

"It looks like you're going to start work, Tom. Isn't that great news?"

Tom's florid complexion changed to a sickly, cheesy colour. Betty went for the jugular.

"Dolly says another reading will give us something more positive."

"Like what?"

"Like the name of the firm . . . That sort of thing."

Tom began to sweat. "Look, Betty luv, how about us coming to an agreement?"

"What do you mean?"

"I'll give up backing horses if you give up visiting Dolly, alright?"

"Agreed. But I'm warning you, Tom Bird: step out of line just once, and back I go to Dolly Varden's for more of her predictions, and you know what that could lead to."

POWER OF THE PUPIL

There always were and always will be bullies. Everyone knows this. They don't usually come in pairs though, not in the same classroom, anyway.

Roland Morley. God! How he hated that name, Roland. The name his mother — just because it was the only link she had with her bachelor brother killed in the Great War — had unthinkingly blessed him with.

Aye, that uncle and his Mam had a lot to answer for. In a time and a place where names like Joe, John, Charlie, Tom, Billy and Bert were commonplace, Roland stood out like a sore thumb.

Then there was his physique. Roland was pencil-thin and, just to make things worse, he had the reddest of red hair possible, which made him a target for numerous, embarrassing remarks such as "Roland, lad, tha looks like a Swan Vesta match" or "Mind when tha takes a bath or thall slip down't plughole" or "I'd stop indoors if it's windy, lad".

But Roland had become somewhat immune to these daily barbs and usually retaliated with one of his own ineffectual ripostes. No, it wasn't these stupid remarks that were distressing; this came from elsewhere.

His headmaster, "Owd" Hector Wainright, and classmate, Charlie "Bully" Bulford were the villains. Wainright verbally so, Bully physically.

However, Roland had a very nimble mind, and this made up for his lack of other assets.

"My time'll come," he used to mutter. And it did.

It all began one dinner break, in the school's playground. Bully Bulford was on the prowl and looking for a victim, and so, too, was Owd Hector Wainright. Hector's mission was to act as peacemaker to any battling duo he happened upon, but it wasn't with good intent. Hector was a boxing fanatic, and his devotion to the sport he generously shared with his class. This was his method.

Any unfortunate couple caught in the act of doing battle were ordered to see him after playtime. Once in his classroom, which was Standard 6, Hector produced from a cupboard two pairs of boxing gloves, which he laced up on two pairs of trembling hands. And today it was the turn of Bully Bulford and Roland Morley.

Wainwright, knowing that Bully never went long before choosing a victim, followed him through the school's wild and raucous kids, out of whom a grinning, swaggering Bully Bulford chose Roland.

On being attacked from behind, and not knowing his assailant's identity, Roland made a swift turnabout to confront him; without a pause, Bully moved in for the kill. And that is when Wainwright intervened.

"Now then, now then, what have we here, eh? Two of my boys fighting at playtime."

45

Bully grinned. "Roland was picking on me, sir. I was just defending myself."

"Is that how it was, Morley? Were you picking a fight with Bulford?"

"Never, sir, I wouldn't do that, sir. I don't fight with anyone . . . Besides he's too big for me, sir."

"You don't have to be big to fight, laddie." He looked at Roland's scrawny frame. "Yes, I really think you could do yourself proud, lad, if you tried hard enough."

Roland began to get worried. All the school knew of Hector's penchant for classroom battles.

"This time, though, I'll let you both off, but don't let it happen again or you'll be in real trouble."

Roland felt a surge of relief, while Bully's chin dropped down to his grubby socks.

Back at their desks, Roland and the rest of the class opened their books in readiness for the next lesson.

"Morley! . . . Bulford! . . . Stand up!" Hector's voice was triumphant. The two lads did as ordered. "These two boys," Hector said, "have broken one of the rules of this school . . . my rule. They have been caught fighting in the playground. Now, class, what happens to anyone caught fighting in the playground?"

A few voices, including an exultant Bulford, answered him. "The gloves, sir, they've got to fight with the gloves, sir."

"That's correct, class, and I will referee, and . . . and the Marquess of Queensberry rules will be adhered to, won't they, class?"

"Yes, sir!" they chorused.

"Right, Morley, Bulford, come forward and face the class."

Opening a tall cupboard, the headmaster took out two pairs of blood-stained boxing gloves, and with some expertise began to lace them up, first on Roland's dithering hands, then on Bully's steady ones.

"Right, laddies, begin whenever you wish. We don't stick to formalities here."

"You're not bloody kiddin', either," thought Roland.

Trapped within the confines of a classroom reverberating with the encouraging chants of its pupils, Roland made a cautionary jab as he circled his smirking opponent. Bulford began to egg him on with provoking taunts.

"C'mon, matchstick, tha can do better than that." Then he made a sudden lunge forward, throwing punches so fast and accurate Roland didn't stand a chance. Wilting under the flurry of blows, Roland was beaten before he started; but it wasn't stopped. Hector's cruel and vicious nature saw to that. There were no three minute rounds, or any Marquess of Queensberry rules either (except for the gloves). No, Hector never called time until blood dripped and tiredness took over, and he loved every minute of it, urging and prompting first one then the other to a better attack or counter-attack.

Eventually, it did come to a stop. Weary arms and buckling legs brought it to a gory end. Bully, too, was exhausted, but without a mark on him.

"I think he's had enough, sir."

"Well, if you think so, we'll call time then, won't we, everyone?"

And all his class were seemingly glad to agree that this one-way punishment should come to an end.

For Roland, that afternoon was the longest and most uncomfortable of his life and he was glad to hear the bell. When questioned by his mother that night, Roland did some lying.

"I've been picked for the rugby team, Mam. It's the first time I've played — enjoyed it, too!"

"Rugby, you? Enjoyed it? That face of yours were never done playing rugby . . . Wait till your dad gets home."

And that's how the true story came out. Under his father's assiduous questioning, Roland broke down and told everything.

"Right!" his dad said. "I'm up to that school tomorrow morning, and Wainright'd better watch out."

"No way, Dad. You'll make me a laughing-stock. Things are bad enough without you doing that!"

"What do you mean, things are bad enough? In what way?"

And Roland told his parents about the ridiculing of his name and physical appearance that he had to endure.

"Well, we certainly can't change your name, but something can be done in t'other department . . . Just you see if it can't."

A week later saw the beginning of the school's six weeks' summer break. On that very same day, Roland's dad came in from work and gave him a large brown envelope. Inside, Roland found a complete course of physical exercises all written and detailed with dozens of sepia photographs of a very muscular Charles Atlas, the author of the course.

"There you are, lad," his dad said. "I want you to start tomorrow on that Charles Atlas course. He also recommends certain diets, you know, to help build you up."

"And are you expecting me to look like Charles Atlas for when I go back to school?"

His dad laughed. "No way, lad, but you'll be stronger and fitter. And there's summat else thall be doing."

"What's that, Dad?"

"I've booked you in Barney The Turk's gym on't common. I reckon some proper boxing will fix you up a treat."

When he returned to school, Roland was fitter and more confident than he'd ever been. There was nothing muscular about him, but his body was harder while also being more supple.

That first day in the playground, Roland went looking for Bully, and the scenario was almost identical. The meeting-up, the challenge, Wainright's intervention, the gloves, and the bloody fight; but this time there was a marked difference. Hector looked on amazed and puzzled as Roland displayed a skill that was mesmerising.

Never again was Roland bullied, but otherwise things didn't change much. Hector still had his perverted enjoyment with other unfortunates. When Roland told his dad — who nearly did handsprings from sheer joy

— he kept a certain idea he'd had to himself. It wouldn't do to disclose everything, would it?

Because he belonged to a Catholic school, Roland was expected — nay, forced — to attend church every Sunday morning, and confession every Friday to confess his wickedness. And one Friday night, Roland did just that, he went to confess his sins and to be absolved. Roland knew by the voice and the facial outline behind the cubicle's curtained grill that the priest was Father Brownlow, noted for his interest in the school's sporting activities. Roland crossed himself. "I want to confess one or two sins, Father."

"Yes, my son, take your time."

"Well first of all, Father, I did a bad thing t'other day. I had a fight with another lad at school."

"To fight to defend yourself is not necessarily a sin, but to turn the other cheek and not to fight is good . . . though it doesn't happen much."

"But I picked on him, Father, knowing that I could beat him."

"In God's eyes, my son, that is wrong. You must learn to be compassionate, to love others as you would love yourself. Violence is wrong."

"That is what Mr Wainright says, Father. He says that fighting should be done sportsmanlike."

"You mean sportsmanlike as in boxing, do you?"

"Yes, Father, he gives us regular instructions in the classroom . . . with boxing gloves, Father."

"That is good. I myself boxed and won many times while training at college."

"Was you that good, Father?"

The priest cleared his throat. "I was very good. I actually won a trophy once, but it taught me to respect my fellow man, and it helps one to prepare for that step into manhood."

"I know this isn't the time or the place, Father, but ... but ..." Roland paused for effect.

"Go on, boy, speak up. There's more to a confessional than being absolved of sin."

"Well, it's like this. Some of the class don't respect Owd ... er ... Mr Wainright's way of doing things ... They don't understand what he's trying to do, that he's trying to help us."

"So the class isn't united, then?"

"No, Father ... and I wonder, Father, since you've done so well at boxing, would you call on us and give us ..."

"To give some clerical instruction in the art of boxing, is that what you have in mind?"

"Yes, Father, that's it, clerical instruction. Everybody will appreciate it, especially our headmaster, and coming from you as well."

"It'll be a pleasure. What time did you say?"

"Can you make it 1.15 prompt, Father, next Monday?"

"Monday, you say?"

"Please, Father. We'll all be very grateful."

Over the weekend, Roland called on his best friend and classmate, Tommy Stubbs, and did some further scheming.

On Monday morning, before the school's whistle, Roland asked permission to use the cloakroom, saying that he felt sick. Once inside the school, Roland, heart beating madly, made his way to his classroom, removed the boxing gloves from the cupboard and stuffed them behind two radiators.

Just before dinner break it began to rain and they were ordered to stay at their desks. And with a warning that rowdy behaviour wouldn't be tolerated, Hector left the room.

Panicking, Roland checked the schoolroom's clock — 12.30. In desperation he went over to Tommy Stubbs's desk and whispered him a slight change of plan.

Lessons resumed at 1 o'clock. Five minutes later, Roland put up his hand.

"Excuse me, sir."

Hector looked up. "Be quick about it, Morley. No lingering."

"I don't want the toilet, sir."

"What is then, Morley? What do you want?"

"It's Stubbs, sir. He's been calling me names, sir, and I've challenged him to a fight, sir."

Hector's face brightened. What better way than a fight to liven up a dull, rainy day? "Come on, then. Get on with it." And he went over to his cupboard.

"Where have the gloves gone? Who's taken the gloves? Come on, own up somebody . . ."

Roland interrupted him. "Excuse me, sir, we don't need the gloves." He turned to Stubbs. "Do we, Tommy?"

Stubbs played his part well and clenched his fists. "Just let me get at him, sir. Just let me."

"Well, if that's what you both want, come to the front and get on with it, then."

Roland glanced at the clock. 1.15p.m. exactly. Perfect.

Keeping their distance, the pair began to throw dummy punches.

"Come on, you two, get on with it, move in. Let's see some action." The class, too, fired by Hector's prompting, began to shout words of encouragement.

And those were the last words that Roland was to hear from the man he hated so much; for right on time, in walked Father Brownlow, a man who had been taught to love and respect his fellow man. And to honour the noble art of boxing, with all its rules and regulations, rules aimed at furthering the cause of respect and comradeship. Bare fist fighting was not, and never would be, a sport. It was a vicious, brutal way of overcoming an opponent. It was a corruption of sporting decency.

Father Brownlow took Owd Hector to one side. The class strained their ears. Roland did manage to make out the words "common street brawling".

A few minutes later, priest and teacher left the room and a replacement was put in charge. It soon came to be known that Hector had been put on indefinite suspension, and while on suspension had a nervous breakdown. And Roland? Well, by the time Owd Hector was fit enough to return to work, Roland had left school and joined the dole queue.

But some good came from this. With time to spare, Roland frequented Barney The Turk's gymnasium and Barney, realising his potential, gave him the backing, the training and the incentive to take that long and arduous path to professional boxing.

DO YOU REMEMBER?

There is no doubt about it: the youth of today have a very hard time avoiding the pitfalls of everyday living.

They are constantly targeted by unremitting advertising. Top-of-the-range mobiles, digital cameras, personal stereos, and designer clothes. And in this commercialised world of advertising, possessions are too easily acquired, which means there is another price to be paid. Young people become bored and disillusioned, and, turn to booze and drugs. But it wasn't like this in the old days.

Back then, people, the working-classes anyway, were thrifty. They had to be. Lack of work and poor wages saw to that.

Even essentials like clothing, footwear and certain kinds of food, like a good cut of choice beef for the weekend, were worried and fretted over, before a final decision was made.

Although most husbands would never admit it, the woman of the house was in sole charge of the purse strings. Every Friday night he would hand over his pay packet and expect very little in return. Perhaps an odd shilling for a pint and a packet of Woodbines, but there was always money put to one side for the rent collector, Christmas club and other necessities.

Mealtimes were so unvaried; you knew what day it was just by looking at your dinner plate. And it was definitely always fish on Friday.

There was always the smell of baking in our house, but occasionally, and I mean occasionally, Mam would produce a decorative tin of assorted biscuits.

And what about entertainment? There were enough silver screens in Wigan town centre alone to keep everybody more than happy. The Ritz, County, Pavilion and the Palace gave us hours and hours of pleasure. Matinees and evening shows, 6 days a week, every week. And just for a change, there was our very own music-hall. The Hippodrome. With a wide range of acts, from real drama to farce, you couldn't go wrong. All honest-to-goodness entertainment; and with not a single Anglo-Saxon, obscene expletive to be heard.

And what about the cigarette smoke in these places? Nearly everyone smoked, especially men. The swirl and drift of the expelled smoke was everywhere. They must have had fantastic ventilation.

Smoking in those days was the working-man's drug. It helped him to relax and take brief respite from the toils and troubles of struggle, especially while watching a good film or having a pint.

These were the hard times of make do and mend. Nothing was thrown away unless it was completely useless.

Clothes, too, were worn to the extremes, and always neatly patched and sewn to extend wearability. Kids' clothing was passed down to the next in line, until, finally, it became too shoddy or unwearable.

If you were lucky enough to wear something new, like shoes or a jacket, there was always a flippant observation to be endured: "Now, mate, what shop did you break into?" Or if it was something that didn't suit some wearer who was passing by, "Look at 'er, that shop must o bin givin' them awa' for free." All said without malice or ill-intent; in days when folk wanted things they couldn't have, but didn't give a damn, and just got on with living the best way they could.

FAG-ASH LIL

John '07

The death of a spouse can result in devastating consequences, and can affect the surviving partner (depending on the circumstances, and the partner) in a variety of ways. This story is just one of them.

Lilian and Billy Sefton, and Billy junior, lived near the bottom of Mayflower Road. Now, situated between their house and Calman's Bone Works was a brickyard, and it was there the local council dumped tons of broken flags and disused cobbles, to be crushed into fine and coarse gravel; and that is where Billy senior worked, on a large and noisy stone crusher.

Back in the forties when work was hard to come by, Billy's job was a secure one, and at that particular time, fairly well paid. As a small family their living standard was quite reasonable; a little restricted perhaps, but they were happy enough. Just about.

The pleasures of Lily and Billy were limited to Billy drinking like a fish (to wash down the gravel dust or so he said), and Lily, well, Lily liked a fag — in fact, she liked a lot of fags and smoked like a factory chimney, and because of her addiction the residents of Mayflower Road gave her the honorary title of Fag-Ash Lil.

For all their indulgences the couple kept a good table, possessed modest but sturdy furniture, and made sure that Billy junior was well shod and decently dressed. You could say it was a marriage made to last. They very rarely quarrelled and, when they did, soon made up. It wasn't exactly a marriage made in Heaven, but stable enough all the same. With his workplace in close proximity, and Lil — who didn't work — keeping the house spick and span and mealtimes on the dot, what else could one wish for?

It was one wintery Saturday night when it all came to an end.

With Billy junior outdoors playing some street game, Lil stoked up the fire, made a cup of tea, lighted another fag and settled down to listen to The Man In Black on the wireless.

A knock on her front door made her curse. The policeman standing there apologised and, after confirming her identity, asked if he could step inside.

"Would you like to sit down, Mrs Sefton?"

Everything about him — his ominous presence, his bulk and the tone of his voice — spoke of doom.

Lil leant against the table. "Why, what is it? . . . What's wrong?"

"I'm afraid it's your husband, Mr Sefton . . . He's had an accident . . ."

"Accident? Accident? Where is he? What's happened? What kind of accident?"

"I'm afraid, Mrs Sefton, your husband is dead."

"Dead? But he can't be! He's gone into town for a drink."

"That's where it happened, as he was leaving the Black Raven pub in the town centre. Apparently he tripped stepping off the curb and fell under the mayor's car. Killed instantly, I'm afraid."

Lil, too shocked to cry, said incredulously, "The mayor's car? Was he driving?"

"The mayor doesn't drive his car, Mrs Sefton. He has a chauffeur to do that for him,"

"But where was the mayor's car going so late on a Saturday night?"

"Apparently he'd just left some sort of function at the town hall, and was on his way home."

Lil took another drag from her umpteenth cigarette of the evening. "What am I going to tell our lad, constable? This'll kill him."

"You'll have to tell him the truth. You can't hide anything like this."

Lil's eyes began to moisten. "Poor Bill, poor lad . . . poor me."

"Would you like me to stay while you fetch the boy?"

"No, no, I think it better if we're alone."

"As you wish, Mrs Sefton," He replaced his helmet and adjusted his cape. "You'll have to make a formal identification, of course, but someone else will be making contact." He touched his helmet.

"Goodnight."

"By the way, constable, how do you know it's my Billy who's been killed?"

"The landlord of the Black Raven, he knew your husband well — very well, in fact."

"Oh, I see. Goodnight, and thank you."

As an only son, young Billy took the death of his father better than expected. The father and son relationship was basically non-existent. As a family they never went on holiday, and when Billy senior had finished a hard day's graft at the brickyard, his only thought after tea was sleep, which he did every evening in his comfortable armchair.

An hour's kip, a wash and brush up, change of clothes, and off he went on his usual pub crawl till closing time. On returning home his son would already be tucked up in bed, and in his own dream world.

His wife Lil, however, took his death very badly. It wasn't just the physical and psychological circumstances of his demise, it was the aftermath. The lack of physical contact, his non-presence, the emptiness . . . the empty purse.

Yes, after a settling-down period came the realisation that with Billy's death her weekly income had also diminished. They had never saved for a rainy day, and now, in her own words:

"How are we going to manage?"

They did manage, just about. A cutback of this, a cutback of that, a cutback of fags! And that is the one thing Lil could not bear, a cutback of that very essential consoling weed. She had smoked too heavily and too long; she just could not do it. Without a fag she too would die. The very thought made her tetchy and unreasonable.

Oh, why, why had her drunken husband fallen under the wheels of the mayor's car and not head first into the stone crusher while doing his job of work? That way she would have been entitled to a trouble-free and reasonable pension for the rest of her days. What luck! What had she done to deserve all this?

With the passing of time, Fag-Ash Lil's fears became a reality, and her daily quota of cigarettes became ever scarcer.

In a desperate attempt to keep puffing, she resorted to the humiliating act of going on the cadge. She would walk the streets or stand at her front door begging from neighbours, passing workmen, even strangers. To satisfy her craving she began to plot and scheme, and Billy junior, who loved his mother and sympathised with her sufferings, became her salvation.

Since time began, women have known that the way to a man's heart . . . and his mind! . . . is through his stomach, and although Billy junior was just a lad, his mother used that same age-old ploy.

It was one Friday teatime when she set her plan in motion. Armed with the biggest dinner plate she could find, she went round to Gregson's fish and chip shop. First in the queue, she ordered a large cod, a double portion of chips, and not one, but two scoops of peas. Then across the road she went to Mrs Weatherall's corner shop and bought the biggest cream cake on display.

Young Billy, just like his dad used to do, rolled up his sleeves and made his attack.

"It's not my birthday, is it, Mam?"

"Don't be cheeky. Course it's not."

"Well, what's the occasion, then?"

"I just thought I'd give you something special, that's all."

"Thanks, Mam, this is really good, thanks."

After tea, with Billy still feeling replete, Lil took a long, deep drag on her cigarette and said, "Do you still love your Mam, Billy?"

"Don't be daft. Course I do."

"Then would you do something special for your mam, lad?"

"Anything, Mam, anything at all."

"I don't like to ask, Billy love, but things are getting really serious."

"What is it, Mam? What do you want me to do?"

"You know I like a fag, don't you, lad?"

"Everybody knows you like a fag, Mam."

"And you know that since your dad died we aint got much money."

"Well?"

"Well, I'd like you to start collecting fag-ends for me."

"Collecting fag-ends?"

"That's right. If you keep your eyes open you'll see plenty on't pavement and in't gutter."

"And you want me to start collecting them?"

"Yes, but don't step in't roadway. I don't want you ending up like your poor dad."

"And what will you do with them?"

"I'll break them open, collect the tobacco, and roll my own."

"That's really desperate, Mam."

"These are desperate times, lad . . . I can buy cigarette papers for next to nothing; they even sell little machines with rollers."

"OK, Mam, I'll do it. Anything for you."

So Fag-Ash Lil — with a lot of help from Billy — went back to being a happy woman. And friends and neighbours gave a sigh of relief.

In those days, long ago, it was a well known fact that Whitsuntide Monday was the day that Roman Catholic schools and churches held their annual walking day. Dressed specially for the occasion, the congregation followed massive banners of their faith. Bands played loud, rousing tunes, and grateful spectators lined the streets to watch and applaud in response to a very moving spectacle.

Now Fag-Ash Lil and Billy were not of the Catholic faith, but Lil persuaded young Billy to take part and join the walkers.

"Just tag on at the tail-end, lad," she said. "Nobody'll know any different, and just imagine the fag-ends you'll find. I mean from start to finish takes hours, all them streets; you'll have a field-day."

Billy wasn't so sure, but when she turned up with a flower for his buttonhole that she had pinched from Wigan Park, the poor lad hadn't the heart to refuse.

Billy was away for four hours, and when he returned he had not one solitary fag-end to his name.

"But what happened, lad? You did walk, didn't you?"

"Course I did, Mam, and I enjoyed it, but I got caught, didn't I?"

"Caught?"

"Aye, Father Brownlow from St. Josephs caught me at it, told me off, made me empty my pockets, asked why I was doing it . . . I had to tell him, Mam."

"Of course you did, lad, that's all right."

"There's something else, Mam."

"Oh?"

"When I'm older he wants me to become a Catholic, and I think I might, Mam. One of me mates is a Catholic; he's an altar boy, an' he's always going on about it."

"That's all right, Billy. You do as you please."

Nevertheless, Billy still did his duty, still collected fag-ends for his mam and even saved up to buy Lil a brand new cigarette-making machine, so that all of his mam's fags were well-packed and uniform in size and shape.

About six months on, Lil's luck once again took an upward turn.

It happened one Monday at midday. A rattle on her front door knocker interrupted her housework. At the door stood a man in overalls; he was holding an inscribed, shiny black flowerpot, the type used in cemeteries.

"Mrs Sefton?"

"Yes."

"I've been asked to call round with this 'ere pot for Billy's grave . . . It's from all of us, his workmates, and bosses . . ."

"And who are you?"

"Fred's me name. I got Billy's job on't crusher."

67

"Oh, you'll have to take care. It can be very dangerous, you know."

"That's all right, I'll not be missed if owt happens, any road."

"Not married, then?"

"No, I reckon I'll always be single. Who'd want somebody like me any road — a labourer on a mucky stone crusher, eh?"

Fag-Ash Lil looked him up and down, took a deep, comforting drag on her cigarette, blew smoke, and said:

"Hmm, would you like a cup of tea? I'm just about to put the kettle on."

DO YOU REMEMBER?

Do you remember when you were growing up? How can you forget?

Especially if, like me, you were brought up in the depression years, when the dole queues were long and money was scarce. I honestly think that when life is hard it leaves you with an indelible memory of the times endured. Not that you resented those times and conditions. How could you? You didn't know any different.

Take for instance the house where me, my two brothers and sister were born and raised. Ours, like many more, had one cold water tap and a shallow brown slop-stone. Until we could afford a geyser, our only means of obtaining hot water was by boiling the kettle. Oh, we had a boiler, a copper one inside a brick surround, with room for a small coal fire underneath. It was situated in a corner, in the back kitchen, and on wash days Mam would make the fire, pile in the dirty clothes and boil them, using a stick to stir the clothes around. Afterwards, the clothes were scrubbed and squeezed through a mangle. That was one of my first jobs after school, turning the mangle for Mam.

When Dad was out of work, Mam took in washing to make an extra shilling or two. It wasn't a nice job, that; not in those days, anyway.

And what about the toilet situation? Our lavvy was a good fifty yards up the backyard. We even had to turn a corner to get there. That meant at night we had to use a chamber pot. Everybody had a po under the bed in those days.

And those bedrooms in winter were like iceboxes. They were colder than any butcher's fridge. It didn't make things any better having to hop across the cold linoleum and down the uncarpeted stairs, either.

Coal was kept under the stairs, and as well as heating the copper boiler it was our only means of heating the living room. And that is where Mam did her baking, on a black-leaded fire range.

On some winter's nights I actually looked forward to when I could spend time in front of a blazing fire, pegging a rug made from sacking and coloured pieces of old, unwanted clothing, like jackets and trousers. It was champion.

By the way, that same fire heated the solid plate oven shelves, which, on a cold winter's night, were wrapped in blankets and used to warm our beds. An unforgettable luxury!

We never had much money, but Dad worked hard — when he was in work — and Mam scraped, saved, baked and slaved to give us the best of what was going. She never seemed to sit down, and when she did she was usually knitting or sewing or darning.

We had some likely characters in our neighbourhood, too. There was Jack Dash, the bookie's runner, built like a whippet, and as fast as one. One Sunday teatime, we had just sat down to a tinned salmon salad, when our front door was flung open. In ran Dash and two of his gambling mates; with breathless apologies, they ran straight through, into the back kitchen, out into the yard and over a wall. Later, we were told they had just managed to escape the clutches of the local bobbies who had broken up their pitch-and-toss school. There are no real characters today, not in our kind of world, anyroad.

I remember our local rat catcher who, with his battle-scarred mongrel dog, spent most of his time at the rat-infested bone works; Jack Pegleg, who would eat anything and never had a stomach problem, and who used to tar his front door every time he tarred his wooden leg; and Father Rimmer, our parish priest who, every Sunday afternoon without fail, would come knocking on the doors of his Catholic congregation, collecting money for the waifs and strays, and if he didn't get an answer he'd go down the entry, walk in the back door and catch us all hiding under stairs and table.

What a life, eh? It was a continual struggle just to keep going, but when the priest came calling he wanted money from an almost empty purse, and, if he caught up with you, you gave it to him. Because there was always somebody worse off than yourself.

Those were the days, eh? Unforgettable.

SNOWY'S FINAL BATTLE

Snowy's life was spectacular, his death bizarre, and the way he died was how it should have been . . .

Just prior to World War Two, our kid and a foreman, who worked for a local roofing firm, were sent on a job somewhere in the wilds of North Wales. The job was a big one: the complete re-roofing of a large farmhouse. Their accommodation was an adjacent barn. And it was there that my brother found a flawless, snow-white kitten that was as wild as the surrounding hills. With great difficulty, and a few scratches to prove it, our kid managed to bring it home to Mayflower Road.

As soon as he came through the door and placed it on our rug, I just knew it was mine.

"Tha'll have to watch out, lad," our kid said. "It'll 'ave thi eyes for sure."

I reached out to stroke it, and was promptly rewarded with four angry-looking scratches the length of my forearm. Mam went berserk, and dashed off to get some ointment. "That thing's not stopping here!" she yelled. "The soddin' thing's wild."

"I couldn't leave it in that barn, Mam," our kid said. "It'd die for sure."

"Oh, it'll die all right if it keeps attackin' Eric, I'll make sure of that."

"I'll tame it, Mam," I said.

"Well, we'll see."

And from that day forward, for the rest of his short but eventful life, Snowy became one of the family. But the testing time had only just begun.

One Friday, after one particularly upsetting incident, everything changed. It was on the very first day school broke up for the summer holidays. As I arrived home, our front door was flung open to reveal Mam gripping Snowy by the scruff of his neck. Giving me one of her murderous looks, she threw the shivering, squealing cat at my feet. "Just in time!" she shouted. "Take that . . . that animal to the canal and drown it." And she slammed the door in my face.

The reason for Snowy's airborne exit was plain to see. The feline's face was covered in its own excrement. Snowy had done his dirt on Mam's carpet and had become the unfortunate victim of her anger.

Tenderly I scooped up the trembling bundle, carried him to Gambler's Field and gently cleaned his face with grass. I had just finished when one of my mates, Birdy Briggs, rode up on his bike.

"Thi mam's just stopped mi, Eric."

"Oh, aye."

"She said to hurry up, thi tays on't table."

"Tell her I don't want any."

"She looks flamin' mad, Eric. She'll not like it."

"Couldn't care less! If I go back the cat comes wi' mi. Tell her that."

Birdy returned with glad tidings, and a truce was called.

With the passing of time, Snowy's attachment to me became, I must admit, annoying. Those summer holidays were all but ruined by his tendency to follow me everywhere. "I wouldn't care," Birdy moaned, "if the soddin' thing wur a dog. At least a dog looks reet." However, a few days later Snowy was to prove to us all that he was a very special cat.

Not far from Mayflower Road there lived a mongrel dog with a formidable reputation. Deep-chested and battle-scarred, Paddy was king of the pack. He was an absolute terror. Just a growl from between those awesome fangs was enough to send the rest running for cover. Black in colour, with a head as big as a lion, this domesticated fighting machine roamed the streets like some prehistoric predator, creating fear and mayhem amongst all four-legged creatures that crossed his path.

We had just turned out, my mate and me, when Birdy noticed that once again Snowy was following us.

"Give mi a minute," I said. "I'll take him back."

As I turned to retrace my steps, I saw in the distance, and heading towards us, the menacing form of Paddy. In a wild state of panic I made a dash for Snowy who, keen to avoid capture, ran in the opposite direction and towards the oncoming mongrel. Paddy, catching sight of Snowy, began to run also. A head-on confrontation was inevitable. With just yards between them, both animals skidded to a stop. A low deep growl came from

Paddy. His hackles rose. The scene was tense. Snowy's tail became erect. There it stood, bristling fiercely, giving it the appearance of some strange albino plant. Then Snowy's back began to arch, and I could almost hear his claws gripping the pavement. I tried enticement. "C'mon, Snowy, kipper time! C'mon, let's go home."

Snowy's response was a blood-curdling feline screech. Then, with claws unsheathed, he made an incredible leap for Paddy's face.

Paddy, the most feared dog for ten square miles, turned tail and ran for dear life and, with Snowy in hot pursuit, vanished round the nearest corner with his tail between his legs.

Jack Calman was proprietor of Calman's Bone and Cowhide Factory which, as everyone knew, was overrun by hordes of rats. One Sunday morning on the last day of our holidays, Jack toured the area sticking up posters. Curious locals gathered in groups to read them. It appeared that Jack was about to demolish a dilapidated wooden workshop to make room for a new brick one. Jack had weighed up the lawful rights and wrongs of such an operation. He knew that, once disturbed, the rats would panic and spill out on to an unmade road that led directly into Mayflower Road. To avoid trouble with the law and the residents, Jack had devised a plan of action, and the posters were his way of giving voice to it. They read thus:

On Sunday 23rd August at 10.10a.m. prompt, the demolition of a disused wooden building at Calman's factory will take place. It is to be expected that a great number of rats will surface. Consequently, I am inviting all dog owners to be on site with their animals at the time arranged. a reward of £5 stirling will be awarded to the owner of the dog with most kills.

Now £5 in 1937 was a fortune, and even dogless families suddenly became dog owners.

The great day arrived. Birdy and me made our way to the rendezvous. The scene was pandemonium. There were dogs everywhere, straining on leashes, growling, barking, snarling and sniffing. Jack Calman arrived. A foreman blew his whistle. The work began. Labourers began to wield sledgehammers and chisels. Rotting timber splintered and shattered. Not one rat showed its whiskered face.

With only the main uprights left standing, it was time to use the crowbars. Suddenly, from the depths of each cavity sprang the very reason for this gathering. Rats!

Dozens scurried forth. The dogs, on being unleashed, went for their prey. What a spectacle! Me and my mate stood rooted in awe and trepidation as the mass of dogs and rats came together, snapping, snarling, biting and worrying, all intermingled with the death-throe squeals of dying rodents.

Suddenly, among the carnage, I saw a flash of white. A cold shiver gripped me. There, side by side among his canine enemies, pouncing and sinking his teeth into furry throats, was Snowy.

Shouts of amazement rose from the crowd. The dogs were the true players in this killing spree, but Snowy held centre stage, and I was proud of him.

However, a few minutes later my pride turned to horror. Cornered amongst a pile of timber, Snowy lost his advantage; several rats retaliated. Dodging dogs and rats alike, I ran to help. Too late! The buggers had gone for Snowy's throat. When me and Birdy arrived on the scene he was already dead.

With eyes brimming, I gathered his still warm body in my arms, and carried him from the melée.

"He was a great cat," Birdy said. "He didn't deserve to die like that."

"Oh aye, he did," I said.

"What do you mean?"

"Snowy never did lose his wild streak, and it wur only fittin' he should go out fightin'."

And with my friend by my side I carried Snowy home, and Mam, who I always thought was as tough as nails, broke down and wept buckets.

The following morning, before school, I washed Snowy clean, wrapped him in one of Mam's old cardigans, left home, followed the canal down to Three Corners Meadow and there, among the dew-soaked grass, dug a deep hole, and laid him to rest.

Back on the towpath I broke into a trot. An hour from now I would be at my lessons; but I knew, without a doubt, that the memory of Snowy's Final Battle, would stay with me forever.

DO YOU REMEMBER?

I remember as a lad — and I don't know why, but it always seemed to be on dark, cold winter's nights — when a bowler-hatted Mr. Harmer, Doctor Berry's man, came calling every Friday about 6p.m. to collect 6 pence (2p in today's money) to cover the whole family for minor medical problems. There wasn't any NHS in those days.

And I also remember Dad and me during the hot summer months, walking down the canal bank to gather a variety of herbs. Plants like dandelion and burdock and nettle from which Dad made dandelion and burdock beer. When it was bottled it had the appearance of today's lager beer; and believe me, it was nectar in a bottle.

And everybody knows the cure for nettle stings; rub a dock leaf on the affected part, and hey presto! The sting disappears. Isn't it strange, the dock plant is always found relatively close to stinging nettle. Back in olden times country folk reckoned that the dock leaf was only effective if the following spell was said simultaneously:

> Nettle Out, Dock in,
> Dock removes the nettle sting.

True or not, it gives the whole idea of herbs and folklore a certain charm and quaintness We also gathered comfrey, which has several common names the most popular one being Knitbone.

Dad would hang the leaves and allow them to dry, and when anyone suffered a strain, bruise or swelling, he would put the leaves in a pan of water and simmer them for about 20 minutes, then the victim would bathe the injured part until relief was obtained.

I remember too, well before the demolition men moved in, and before communities were scattered, neighbours, especially the wives of injured pitmen, knocking on our front door and asking Dad for a few leaves of Knitbone to treat their husband's or son's knocks and bruises received while working a shift.

But in those days, even if you didn't know your herbs, there was always an herbalist shop within easy walking distance where you could buy, for a few coppers, any herb for any complaint under the sun; all nature's remedies, which, with a bit of knowledge, could be gathered personally from local fields and meadows.

And do you remember too, friendly neighbours nipping next door to make cinder tea for a newborn baby with the gripes? When money was short, which was often, they couldn't afford gripe water, so they made cinder tea. And this is how it was done.

Take a red hot cinder out of the fire, put it in a cup of cold water, let it stand for a few seconds, put in some sugar, let it stand some more, sieve it into another cup, cool it again, then pour it into the baby's feeding bottle. That got the wind up, I'll tell you!

So, if you fancy reviving an age-old remedy for gripes, why not have a go? And if you can do this with a modern gas fire, write it down, get it published and you'll make a fortune.

Now the humble potato, as everybody knows, is not a herb, but a vegetable. But it was once thought that a stolen potato was a useful charm against rheumatism, and would be carried in a pocket or around the neck. And warts rubbed with a potato would disappear as the vegetable rotted.

Personally, I like my spuds on a plate, chipped, boiled or mashed, or made into a belly-filling hash.

ANOTHER DUNKIRK
MIRACLE

I was still at school when cousin John "Ginger" Dyson went to war. But I remember it well. Actually, John had sandy coloured hair, but his schoolmates, even the teachers, called him Ginger, and he was stuck with it for the rest of his days.

Apart from his noticeable, unruly mop of hair, Ginger was tall, well-built and athletic. As a schoolboy, he was awarded many a cup and shield for both boxing and swimming, but mostly for swimming; a sport that, with the passing of time, became a pleasant pastime. And our local canal which ran parallel to Mayflower Road became the venue for many a watery, friendly competition between friends . . . and even enemies.

The distance from Elston Bridge to Wigan Pier was approximately one mile, and the competitors would line up on the edge of the wooden structure, wait for a signal — usually from a non-swimmer — dive off and, using a stroke of their choice, swim like the clappers for the pier.

Ginger always won, but he wasn't a braggart. That's why the rest accepted defeat. It was quite satisfactory coming in second to Ginger's first, and that's what the rest tried for; coming second to Ginger Dyson was an honour indeed.

On leaving school, Ginger didn't join the dole queue. He left school on a Friday, and on the following Monday he took a walk along the canal towpath. Arriving at Paxton Locks, he helped a lone boatman to open the lock gates, asked him for a job, and got it.

It was a job, and a friendship, that lasted until, on his seventeenth birthday, he decided to join the Territorial Army, with the intention — if all went well — of eventually joining the regular army. However, all this planning for his future came to nothing. Oh, he became a soldier alright, and he fought, and he survived. Just about!

On the day Ginger went down to the Territorial Drill Hall to sign up he met, to his surprise, an old school mate, who also lived in Mayflower Road but quite a few doors away from Ginger. In build and mannerisms they were complete opposites. Against Ginger's broad, athletic bulk and steadiness, Donald Lathom was small, wiry, quick and provocative; but as individuals, they went together like bread and butter.

After signing the necessary papers and receiving a pending medical examination date, they made off to the nearest public house for a pint and a pork pie.

Now, Ginger, and everyone else, knew that Donald could not hold his drink. Two or three pints and Donald was on the lookout for trouble. But Ginger, because the occasion warranted a celebration, overlooked his friend's incapacity to absorb alcohol, and later, after four pints of strong stout, regretted his lack of common sense.

An accidental nudge from a fellow-drinker at the bar, and a spill of beer, was enough to ignite Ginger's fiery friend and, when Ginger returned from emptying his bladder, Donald was just dodging a ham-like fist from an equally intoxicated opponent. Ginger stepped between them, and took a blow on his right ear. With a curse from pain and frustration, Ginger brought his pugilistic know-how into play and, blocking a follow-up, struck the unfortunate stranger on his fleshy chin with a perfect right-hander, sending him staggering back, down and out, at the feet of several boozers.

Threatened with police intervention, Ginger and Donald, with a wave to the landlord, made a hasty exit.

They got on well, did the duo, and as often happens to men in uniform, their friendship grew ever closer and stronger. But one day in 1939 those enjoyable Territorial days came to an abrupt end. With the outbreak of World War Two, Ginger and Donald were just two of the 158,000-strong British Expeditionary Force to be shipped across the channel to France. And, some weeks later, followed a humiliating retreat.

Chased by 750,000 Germans, and caught up in some desperate rearguard action, the two friends came face to face with the true horrors of war.

Hundreds of soldiers and civilian refugees had been killed trying to escape along the congested roads. Burnt-out lorries and abandoned equipment lay everywhere. At one point they became separated from their unit and decided to go on alone. It was that or be killed or captured by the advancing Germans.

When they reached Dunkirk, the scene was one of utter chaos. Bodies in bloodstained surf, damaged and burning tanks and jeeps. Any transport not already damaged was being destroyed.

Farther back from the shoreline, troops were scattered everywhere; some were taking refuge in sandy dug-outs, others just lying in the dunes, seemingly confused and disorientated, waiting for someone to take command. Shells from warships offshore whined and whistled overhead.

Ginger and Donald took shelter in a vacant hole in the dunes. However, having had nothing to eat for hours, Donald decided it was time to do some foraging. As he left the hole a bomb or shell — Ginger never knew what — landed close by, killing his friend instantly, and causing a searing, burning and intense pain in his left arm and down the left side of his body. Ignoring the pain, Ginger scrambled over to his friend, but could do nothing. He then did the only thing possible. Taking Donald's name tags from around his neck, he struggled over to an abandoned lorry, found a spade, and buried his mate deep in the sand, then marked the spot with his rifle.

After a while, the burning pain and discomfort began to subside and, so encouraged, he went down to the beach to join a painstakingly slow-moving line of bedraggled, cursing soldiers that stretched way out to sea and the waiting boats and ships of every description. With water up to his chest, the wait for him lasted twelve hours, as various vessels left with their human cargo. At last, on the point of collapse, he was hauled aboard a small boat and given food and drink; he then slept deeply all the way to Blighty.

Once on British soil, Ginger reported Donald's death to the authorities, and his makeshift burial spot and, of course, his own, painful, seeming non-injury. After a thorough examination nothing serious could be physically identified, and it was then that Ginger decided to apply for a transfer; in fact, a change of uniform. The carnage at Dunkirk was the deciding factor. Anyway, one Dunkirk miracle, in one lifetime, was quite sufficient, thank you very much.

And so he volunteered for the Mercantile Marines, whose job was to provide safe passage for ships passing through the English Channel, which were indispensable for the essential supplies and the morale of Great Britain. German U-boat commanders, however, had other ideas, and Ginger was shipwrecked twice.

It was after these disasters that his so-called non-physical problem returned, and he once again began to experience pain and numbness from his left shoulder down to his left foot — a numbness that eventually forced him, reluctantly, to drag his foot. And neither could he grip anything with his left hand, forcing him to report sick, because of which a subsequent medical examination board deemed him unfit for military service of any kind.

Back home in Mayflower Road, Ginger spent his time in idle contentment. However, but for his incapacity Ginger would have enjoyed his forced retirement even more. Although a full army pension was some consolation, it didn't compensate for the healthy lifestyle he once enjoyed.

Slowly, irrevocably, Ginger's condition worsened. Then one day, just on the spur of the moment, and for a brief time only, the John "Ginger" Dyson of old returned, and everyone in Mayflower Road knew that somewhere, deep down, he was still the same man who had gone to war. His physical affliction would never undermine his courage or his determination to rise above adversity.

It was a very hot and humid Sunday afternoon, and our local canal was teeming with swimmers of all ages. Gambler's Field, too, was alive with people taking advantage of the good weather.

Ginger and a fellow boozer, Sam Colley, left the Three Crowns pub at closing time, and they, too, decided to join the happy revellers.

Ginger, because of his condition, always put a limit on his liquid intake, but Sam was on holiday and was feeling in a laddish mood. When they arrived on Gambler's Field he decided to cool off and, seeing a gap among the carefree swimmers, took a mighty leap, and landed, fully clothed, smack in the middle of them. The trouble was, Sammy couldn't swim, and began to struggle and go under.

Without a pause, and moving with some long-dormant alacrity, Ginger stripped to his waist, dived in and pulled Sammy, gasping and struggling, to the side, where many willing hands dragged them onto the bank and safety.

At teatime that night, Mam happened to mention the incident, and asked Dad how on earth a severely handicapped man like Ginger Dyson had managed to save the drunken Sammy from drowning.

And Dad put it in a nutshell, when he said, with great pride:

"That, my love, is what you might call another Dunkirk miracle."

A STITCH IN TIME

John '07

I left school in the summer of 1945 aged fourteen, when our wartime hero, Winston Churchill, was rejected as a peacetime leader and his successor, Clement Attlee, announced that a period of austerity lay ahead. And boy, was he right.

For the time being, however, my escape from a school that taught me very little was a euphoric occasion and, because of the headmaster's ruling that only short trousers should be worn by all pupils, my first pair of long ones was an added bonus.

For the first two weeks, Mam gave me the freedom of the streets, then one particular Monday morning gave me a gentle hint that it was time to start looking for work; and that was the problem.

I had this urge to be a carpenter, but numerous visits to the dole office and applications to various firms proved fruitless. My desire to become a full-time chippy came to nothing.

It was Dad who first saw the advert, and I remember it was on a Friday evening after tea. He shook out the evening paper, crossed his legs, and from the comfort of his fireside chair read the following:

Benjamin Bristow and Son, makers of saddlery and fine leather goods, require young, willing apprentice. Good prospects guaranteed. No references required.

Dad put down the paper, gave me a triumphant look, and said:

"By 'eck, that's just the thing, Eric. It won't be much money, but it's a trade . . . not far to travel, either."

"Where is it?" Mam said.

"Why, near't town centre, not far from bus station."

"That's only about fifteen minutes walk, and no bus fares, either," Mam said. "And like your dad said, it's a trade: you'll be set up for life."

"How about it, Eric?" Dad said.

"I suppose so . . . but if I don't like it I'm not stoppin'."

"I'll come with you, if you want," Dad said.

"Not flamin' likely. What do you think I am, a flamin' kid?"

"Better make it quick then, lad: I bet they're queuing up for a job like that."

"Aye, I bet they are. Anyroad, I'll go Monday mornin' early."

"They'll be open tomorrow, you know. It's that sort o' business."

"I'll go Monday," I said defiantly.

"Please thisel."

On Monday, at 10 o'clock sharp, hair neatly parted and slicked back and shiny shoes gleaming black from

Mam's assiduous polishing, I made my way through the sun-warm streets.

I was dreading this interview and hoped and prayed that the job had been taken. The closer I got to my destination, the slower I walked. Then, inevitably, I arrived. The name and business displayed outside read just like the advertisement, with just one addition:

ESTABLISHED 1899

The building was low, nondescript and whitewashed, and situated well away from other shops and businesses. I entered.

A long wooden counter with a hinged flap barred my way. All was quiet.

"Hello! . . . Is there anyone . . . ?"

From a dimly lighted rear, a small, stout, bespectacled man, wearing a brown apron across his ample belly, came forward.

"I've come about the job."

He smiled. "I'm Mr Bristow. I own the place." He lifted the flap. "Come through, will you?"

The pungent smell of leather was almost overpowering. The workshop was untidy. In the centre was a pot-bellied stove, with a tubular chimney going through the ceiling. On the far wall were three unattended wooden benches, littered with an assortment of unfamiliar tools and unfinished work: an aged saddle, a pair of battered, leather trousers (the kind worn by speedway riders) and an expensive-looking brown handbag.

I followed him into a small office on the left. Once behind his desk he gave me a searching look and smiled. But he didn't smile with his eyes, which were close-together little piggy eyes. He indicated a chair.

"Sit down, laddie . . . sit down. What's your name, by the way?"

"Eric, sir."

"No need to call me sir, Eric. Mr Bristow will suffice."

"Thank you, Mr Bristow."

"Now, Eric, what school did you go to?"

"St. Josephs."

"You mean the Catholic school close to Wigan Pier?"

"Aye, that's the one."

"And do you attend church on a regular basis, Eric?"

"We had to, Mr Bristow. T'headmaster saw to that."

"And now you've left school will you continue to attend?"

"I don't think so."

"Why not?"

I shrugged. "I've done enough church goin' to last me a lifetime."

"I go to church, Eric, regularly . . . No one forces me, I just know it's the right thing to do."

Things were getting serious. I shrugged again. "I'll probably keep it up. Mam and Dad'll probably make me go anyway."

"Good lad. Now, how's your reading and maths?"

I thought I'd better do some more lying: "Top o' the class, Mr Bristow." I hoped to God he wouldn't test my mathematical skills.

"Good. Now then, when can you start?" He seemed very keen to take me on.

"Is there no one else in for the job then?" I said, hopefully.

"No, Eric, you're our first applicant."

"Just my bloody luck," I thought.

He rummaged around in his desk drawer and drew out some official-looking forms.

"How about starting next Monday? We open at 8:30; that gives us time to get organised for a 9 o'clock start."

"8:30?"

"Yes, and I do appreciate good timekeeping. Understand?" He gave me two of the forms. "In the meantime, ask your father to fill these in."

The following Monday at 8:15 prompt I was welcomed by a grumpy Bristow and ordered to make a fire in the pot-bellied stove. I gave him the forms Dad had filled in and signed, and set to work. Kindling wood, newspaper and coal were kept in a metal box at the stove's base. With great difficulty and underbreath cursing, I managed at last to get the thing going. My next task was to sweep the floor and tidy the workbenches littered with odd-shaped, razor-sharp knives and tools. Then I was shown how to beeswax lengths of thread used for stitching leather.

Later, over tea and biscuits, he gave me a general idea of what my working day would be. Mornings would be spent similarly to this one, cleaning up, and tidying benches. Afternoons I would spend learning the trade — small stitching jobs on leather off-cuts; riveting and intricate tooling would also be on the agenda.

He pointed to a bench on the far side of the workshop.

"You'll be using that bench over there. The one next to it is mine, as that way I'll be able to keep an eye on your progress . . . and the other one is Vernon's."

"Vernon?"

"My son, my only son. He's on holiday just now . . . He'll be back tomorrow." He sighed and shook his head slightly. "I hope."

I sensed that all was not well between them. "Do I call him Vernon, Mr Bristow?"

"Yes, yes, Vernon won't mind . . . He doesn't mind much about anything, does our Vernon, and you will find that he's quite demanding."

Vernon Bristow was the complete opposite to his father. Slight of build, with a good head of brown hair that topped a somewhat thin, crafty-looking face, but a likeable person all the same.

His first demanding request was made at midday. A tin of snuff and two cold pork pies from a nearby butcher's shop, which he devoured sat at his bench scanning the day's race meetings.

One thing I did notice was that, while his father's work entailed saddlery and harness and general repairs, Vernon concentrated on the more exclusive leather goods: elegant handbags, purses and wallets, some of them made to customers' specifications.

And me, well, apart from easing myself slowly into this world of leather, I was also the errand lad.

One Friday afternoon, Vernon handed me a brown paper parcel containing a beautifully made shoulder-bag, with a delivery address in the grander part of town. So, with enough bus fare safe in my pocket, I set off.

Number 3 Armitage Way was set in its own grounds, well away from the bustle and noise of passing traffic, and stood large and imposing at the end of a long driveway, bordered by mature trees and shrubs. Feeling somewhat insignificant in the grandeur, I rang the bell. A tall handsome woman dressed in a plain black frock answered my ring.

"Mr Bristow . . . Vernon Bristow asked me to deliver this parcel, Miss . . . Mrs . . . erm . . ."

She smiled briefly: "Come in, young man. Would you like a glass of lemonade or something?"

"No, thanks, I have to be getting back."

"Are you sure? Anyway, just bear with me. I'll only be a moment."

She left the door ajar. I watched as she went to a table in the hallway and opened the parcel. With scarcely a glance at the exquisite leatherwork, she opened the bag and took out what appeared to be several cellophane packets, and in these packets were — what seemed to me anyway — silk stockings, and even I knew that silk stockings, and many other things in 1945, could only be obtained on the black market.

My heart missed a beat. The woman, now smiling broadly, and with a jaunty step, returned. "Tell Vernon I am delighted with the goods; he's done a wonderful job. Tell him that, will you? And this is for you." She shoved a threepenny bit into my sweaty hand. "Goodbye," she said, and closed the door.

Benjamin Bristow seemed overly concerned with my personal life, and one day began to really delve deep. "You don't smoke or swear, do you, Eric?"

"No, Mr Bristow."

"And remember, Eric, even when you're old enough, never take to drink. It's the ruination of man . . . in every sense."

"I won't, Mr Bristow."

"And what about girls? Do you have a girlfriend?"

"No, Mr Bristow."

"Still going to church, are you?"

"Of course, Mr Bristow."

"What kind of friends do you have, Eric? . . . I mean, are they good and decent lads you knock about with?"

"Aye, of course they are."

"Have you or any of them ever been in trouble with the police?"

This was getting weird. "Why do you want to know that, Mr Bristow?"

"Just a fatherly concern, lad. While you're working for me I'll be responsible for your welfare, and your progress . . . you're one of the family now."

I wondered what Dad would have to say about that.

A while later, little stickers began to appear at certain strategic places, especially in the toilet.

"FLEE FROM THE WRATH TO COME!"

"GOD IS EVERYWHERE"

"TRUST IN THE LORD"

I was hoping for some kind of reaction from Vernon, but Vernon had other things on his mind.

For weeks, Vernon had been hard at work making a small attaché case, and I watched spellbound as leather, locks, hinges, studs, amazingly neat white stitching and also, just to give it even more quality, a deep green cloth lining became the finished product. And on the lid, in gold inlaid lettering, was the name JOHN C. BRANDON. Vernon then gave me the job of giving it a final polish.

For days the case stood on a shelf until, finally, a week later, I realised the case had gone. That same day Vernon called me over to his bench.

"I want you to do another errand for me, Eric." He gave me another brown paper parcel. "I want you to deliver this attaché case to the same address as last time. It's for Mrs Brandon's husband, John. They're old friends and I do special jobs for them, you see."

I took the parcel somewhat gingerly. "I'll need some bus fare, Vernon."

"I want you to use the bike. Dad's complaining about the time it takes using buses. And by the way, be careful. You'll find the case a little heavy; I've packed it with cardboard. OK?"

"I'll take good care of it, Vernon," I said confidently.

"You can have your dinner before you go. That way you should get to their house about 1:30. You'll have plenty of time to check the bike over — you know, tyres and things."

"Does Mr Bristow know where I'm going?"

"Er, no, dad won't be in today, and when you leave I'll be closing up. I've an urgent appointment in town, so don't hurry back. OK?"

And sure enough, just as I was putting the parcel in the bicycle carrier, Vernon gave me a curt nod and left.

Later, after a ten-minute chat to an out-of-work mate I, too, set off. At that time of day the roads were fairly busy and when I reached the town centre there was a bobby on point duty directing traffic. He gave me the halt signal for a few minutes, then beckoned me forward. I went onwards with a wobble, but at that moment I saw, on the opposite side of the road, Vernon and a shady-looking character entering the Black Horse public house. I wobbled even more. Next minute, a car that seemed to come from nowhere crashed into me. I managed to fall without injury, and struggled to my feet, but Vernon's parcel was in tatters under one of the front wheels of the car. The case, too, had burst open to reveal the contents. But not cardboard, as Vernon had mentioned, but those now-familiar cellophane packets of nylons, and chocolates, and cigarettes and . . .

"What's this lot, then?"

It was the policeman, and he was eyeing me up with a look that only suspicious policemen can give.

"I think you'd better accompany me down to the station, laddie."

At the police station, consoled with tea and biscuits, I told my story. The case was confiscated. I was told to go home, that I might be required as a witness at a later date, and that Vernon would have an official call the following day.

And that call, by a tenacious, young constable, eliminated suspicions of wrong doings on my part.

Vernon was found to be entirely innocent of any unlawful misdemeanours. After all, it was quite legal to supply his friends, the Brandons, with gifts that were extremely scarce in those years of austerity, and with me acting as postman . . . Well, end of story.

Not long after, I decided that I wanted a change, something with more of a challenge. After nine months of riveting, tanning, and stitching, it was time to move on. Time to leave it behind, and remember it all as just . . . *a stitch in time* . . . So to speak.

DO YOU REMEMBER?

Times change, people change, habits change; and one big change that has affected millions, is leisure time, especially holidays.

Today, millions spend their holidays in the sweltering heat of foreign lands: Spain, Malta, Africa, the Caribbean Islands, and Florida, you name it, and it is visited. Cruises, too, and adventure holidays are very popular. But it's not always been so.

For the first 2 weeks of every July, the noise and bustle of Wigan's cotton mills fell silent. Other industries, too, either closed their doors or kept going with a reduced workforce. Even a few shops put up their shutters.

And where did these hard-working folk go on holiday? Blackpool, Southport, Rhyl, Llandudno, and various other destinations, were invaded by hopeful, sun-seeking, fun-loving, thirsty and hungry holiday-makers, who were the town's working-classes.

They travelled by train, bus or charabanc. If you stayed at home the town was deserted, so, to break the monotony, you booked a day trip by charabanc.

The coach firms of Smiths, Barnes, and other companies did a roaring trade. Those well-upholstered, colourful but cramped single-deckers took a route that included a stop at some tiny rural cafe — there were no motorways those days — then off again to the seaside resorts of Wales, and not forgetting Scarborough, Morecombe, and, of course, the favourite, Blackpool. And there was one thing for sure, whichever resort you visited, you were certain to bump into someone you knew: workmates, neighbours, distant relatives, even your boss.

"How do, Joe, where et stoppin'?"

"Why, it's Sammy Fisher, how long art 'ere fer, mate?"

"Hello, Molly, luv, ha thowt thee an' Billy were gooin' to New Brighton."

All good friends, out to have a good time best way they could, and even these familiar, well-known faces weren't going to stop them. Then the hunt for a good fish and chip shop or cafe, followed by a visit to the nearest crowded bar for a couple o' gills and just to cool things down, a paddle in the sea before tea.

Now a Christmas holiday was different. For a start it was obviously colder, and it didn't last very long. But Christmas is a time for family gatherings, and receiving and giving gifts. But the kids of today get that many presents their bedrooms look like Aladdin's caves. And not cheap stuff either. Automated toys, Game Boy games, top-of-the-range bicycles, televisions, computers. If they want it, they get it.

Where will it all end? And what will the kids of today be giving the kids of tomorrow?

The mind boggles.

We, the kids of yesterday — the poor ones anyway — didn't get a lot for Christmas. And with money being scarce there were no comparisons to make. A mouth-organ, a torch, a spinning top and whip, a few lead soldiers, and, if your parents thought you were up to it, the latest *Pears' Cyclopedia*. And for Dad, a white silk scarf or cardigan, handkerchiefs or tie. Take your pick; you couldn't have them all.

Those were the days when money and possessions were hard to come by. You didn't dictate the type of present you wanted, you were always happy with what you had been given, and thought nothing of it. What you got, you cherished, and, being happy with your lot in life, you thought yourself the luckiest kid in the world.

THOSE WILD ACCORDION DAYS

The writing of this story brought back many happy memories. Happy days of pub entertainments, warm beer, tinkling pianos, crooners and tenors — and best of all, those wonderful accordions.

We were just eighteen, Wilf and me, when it all began, and on reflection it all began with the untimely death of Wilf's father.

Having been schooled together, Wilf Doxy and me now worked together. Blake's Cotton Mill stood proud and imposing, not far from Wigan Pier. Apart from numerous cotton mills, coalmines, too, were the lifeblood of Lancashire's working classes; and that is where Wilf's dad met his maker, buried under a mass of rock and coal.

Mr Doxy's funeral was an exceptional and sad occasion. Two things accounted for this.

First and foremost, it highlighted once again the dangers of working underground.

Secondly, the death of Billy Doxy, a talented accordionist, left a silent void in the world of local entertainment.

But his send-off was spectacular. Fans, neighbours, friends and fellow artists thronged the streets. Some shed copious tears, others made light of the occasion.

"I can see owd Billy up theer now, playing away on 'is owd accordion."

"You daft sod," his companion said. "They don't play accordions up theer, they only play 'arps."

"Not Billy Doxy. There's only angels play 'arps, an' Billy were no angel."

"Oh shuddup, an' take thi cap off. T'hearse is comin'."

With Billy now gone his wife, Annie, a dedicated Catholic, applied for work at Blake's Mill and was given a job in the winding-room. A week later she filled a barmaid's vacancy at the Three Crowns pub in Mayflower Road.

One day at work, Wilf told me all about it. "Mi mam's drivin' mi potty, Eric."

"You mean because of what's 'appened?"

"Sort of. She wants mi to step into Dad's shoes."

"I don't like the sound of that."

"Don't be funny, Eric."

"Sorry."

"Have you any idea why she's taken on all this work, eh?"

"It 'as got mi wonderin'."

"So that I can take up accordion lessons, that's why."

"I thowt tha could play already. Didn't thi dad show thi?"

"That's reet, but Mam wants mi to 'ave some style, just like Dad had."

"No 'arm in that, mate."

"She wants mi to carry on where Dad left off."

109

"You mean doin' pubs and clubs?"

"That's it, mate."

With Annie's barmaid work came the advantage of position. In other words, six months after Wilf's tutorials began, she convinced her boss, Jerry Colman, that Wilf was now in the same league as her late husband. The landlord, keen to fill the void — and his pub — decided to take the risk.

Suffering the agonies of a first-night performance, Wilf asked me to accompany him. The night was incredible. The tenor singer was excellent, the crooner, top-notch; but it was the rousing singsongs to the tunes on Wilf's accordion that brought the house down. "And his solo playing," someone said, "was like the reincarnation of Doxy senior."

The future looked promising, for mingling amongst the revellers were several landlords and club concert secretaries. From that night on, Fridays, Saturdays and Sundays became a cycle of glorious entertainment.

Mrs Doxy, bathing in the glow of Wilf's success, was a happy woman; but a drastic change was imminent.

When Jenny Boardman, a new starter at Blake's, came into our lives, everything changed. Pretty, and well-proportioned, with a mysterious air of shyness, she at once drew the attention of all male employees, especially Wilf. He was besotted.

A week after their first meeting, he began to court her. And while his love interest grew more fervent, his bookings went into slow decline. Giving me the embarrassing task of making cancellations, he gradually, but ruthlessly brought those wild accordion days to an end.

Mrs Doxy took this change in Wilf's lifestyle very badly. All her hard work and planning had come to nothing.

But even amongst the chaos of disruption and disappointment I was always invited to tea on Sundays. It was on one of these visits that a head-on clash between mother and son really brought the shutters down.

We had just finished eating when Wilf dropped his bombshell.

"By the way, Mam," he said, "I'm saving up to get married."

Mrs Doxy shrugged her shoulders. "Couldn't care less. Why tell me about it?"

"Because you're mi mother, that's why."

The atmosphere was tense. I began to feel like an intruder. I stood up.

"Well, thanks for the meal, Mrs Doxy." But Mrs Doxy wasn't listening.

"Some son you've turned out to be."

"Now mother, there's no need for this."

"Uh!"

"But you've never met Jenny. You don't know her."

"I know of her . . . and I've heard she's a Protestant."

"So, you've been goin' behind mi back, 'ave you?"

"People talk."

"Bloody gossips!" Wilf snapped.

"And do you think she'll give up her religion to marry you? Uh?"

I moved closer to the door.

"Your poor father'll be spinning in his grave."

"What for? Because I'm goin' out wi' a Protestant?"

"You know why."

Wilf leapt to his feet and grabbed his coat. "I've had enough of this. C'mon, Eric, I'm off."

Shortly after their flare-up, Wilf moved in with his Auntie Mildred, Annie's sister.

A few weeks later, Jenny developed a wracking cough, and a gradual loss of weight. A visit to the doctor and a subsequent visit to the chest clinic confirmed the doctor's diagnosis: she had tuberculosis, and was speedily admitted to a T.B. sanatorium.

Three weeks passed before I made my first visit, and with Wilf — who was a regular visitor — made the twenty-mile bus journey one wintery Sunday afternoon.

When we arrived the pair of us nearly died from shock. Mrs Doxy was seated by Jenny's bed, chatting and fawning over her like a favourite aunt. She looked up as we entered and beamed a smile of indulgence. "I was just telling Jenny, think positive, trust in God, and she'll soon be home . . . Isn't that right?"

Wilf and I were left speechless.

From that day on a truce was called, and Wilf returned home.

Miraculously, Jenny survived her ordeal and was given a clean bill of health.

The next Sunday get-together was a real revelation. The three of us — Wilf, Jenny and me — were treated in the true spirit of forgiveness and reunion. Mrs Doxy had even purchased a bottle of expensive fine sherry. But there was a bigger shock to come.

With the meal over and the pots washed and stowed away, Mrs Doxy refilled our glasses.

"I would like to make a toast," she said. And looking fondly at the happy couple, she continued, "To Jenny and Wilf on their coming engagement."

A stunned silence followed as her words sank in.

"You'll 'ave to wait a bit, Mam . . . till I've saved some money, that is," Wilf said.

"I'll give you the money."

"We can't take your money, Mrs Doxy," Jenny said. "It wouldn't be fair."

"Don't you worry, I won't be paying for the ring. That wouldn't be right, would it?"

"I'll make sure you get every penny back, Mam," Wilf said.

"No need for that, just the ring'll do . . . But I do want you to do one special thing for me."

"Just you name it," Wilf said happily.

"On the day of your engagement I want you to play your accordion."

"I don't see why not. What do you say, Jenny?"

"I think it's a great idea. Besides, I've never heard you play — I'm looking forward to it."

One month later the Three Crowns concert room was packed to capacity with friends and relatives from both families. With the buffet consumed, the entertainment began. Down to his shirt sleeves, Wilf was on form. He played his heart out, and the gleam in his eye spoke volumes.

Naturally, there were people present who were complete strangers to me. One of them, a big man smoking a fat cigar and dressed in expensive clothes, spent quite some time in a deep conversation with Mrs Doxy. "He must be from Jenny's side," I thought. Later I gave voice to my ponderings.

"That big chap, Mrs Doxy — is he one of Jenny's relations?"

Slightly tipsy, and flushed with pleasure, Mrs Doxy smiled a smile of contentment.

"That gentleman, Eric, is Mr Strong. He's a freelance promoter. He scouts around for new talent and finds them work."

"Work?"

"You know — radio, theatre, cabaret, that sort of thing."

"And?"

"He thinks that lad o' mine's got real class. He's very impressed."

She touched her lips with a forefinger. "Shh . . . Don't tell our Wilf, will you Eric? . . . He'll swear I've planned it all."

I looked across the room. Wilf, with sweat running down his face, elbows and fingers on the go, a passion in his eye, and no Jenny in sight, was on cloud nine.

"How could anyone even think of stifling such talent, Eric?"

I smiled, and knew without a doubt that her scheming and planning had brought back the thing she wanted most: those wild accordion days.

DO YOU REMEMBER?

Do you remember before the demolition men moved in, and whole communities had to move out?

I was born and bred in a part of Wigan where trust, compassion and comradeship went hand in hand, when a knock on a neighbour's front door didn't warrant an answer; you lifted the latch, walked right in, sat down, accepted a cup of tea and had a good natter.

Where are they now, these friends and neighbours? Scattered like seeds on barren ground, pressing TV remotes and remembering the past. Remembering those carefree Sunday, childhood jaunts along the canal to Gathurst, armed to the teeth with jam butties and bottles of tap water — I can still see those breadcrumbs floating around in those bottles. Then the walk home, sun-tanned, tired and starving, to be greeted with the mouth-watering aromas of Mam's scrumptious home-made bread and cakes and pies and, of course, custard, blancmange and jelly. And after tea, back outside playing street games until dusk; followed by a thorough scrub-down at the slop stone, then up the wooden hill to bed. How can you ever forget where you were born and bred? Where neighbours loved, cried, laughed, married and died.

I remember old Jem Fisher, the rag-and-bone man, and Jimmy, his little faithful horse, who, one hot summer's day collapsed between the shafts of his cart. Jem cried his heart out, and Jimmy spent the rest of his days cropping grass on a nearby field.

And I remember a snuff-taking mystic neighbour who read tea leaves and once made a prediction that the husband of one of her clients would lose a leg. On Christmas Eve, he nipped into the Three Crowns pub, had one too many, and left all of his shopping — including the nice leg of lamb — in the snug. He never did get that leg back!

I will never forget that place of refuge, the Three Crowns, where local entertainers helped us — if only for a short while — to forget our trials and tribulations. Paddy on the piano, Harry, tenor solo, and Mavis, soprano. And my mate Wilf, the finest accordionist for miles around. By 'eck, could he play.

Every Saturday night I, his friend for life, played an important role in this world of entertainment. In between satisfying drinks of lovely complimentary beer, I would strenuously turn the pages of his music while Wilf, down to his shirt sleeves and tie undone, rattled out all the favourite tunes of the day: "Danny Boy", "Just a Song at Twilight", "Bless this House" and so on. And when time was called, a finale of singsongs.

Then on the way home, a call for fish and chips, followed by some raucous street singing.

Then home to bed. What a night, eh?

GOODBYE, WIGAN PIER

Greenwood's shop, not far from Wigan Pier, was owned and run by Isaac Greenwood and his wife, Frances. The shop had two windows, one on each side of the front door. The one on the left displayed various signs that advertised the goodness of Cadbury's Dairy Milk Chocolate, tea, coffee, hot or cold Vimto and other soft drinks that would accompany freshly made sandwiches, and hot or cold pies.

The window on the right was of a more sombre nature, expressing the healing qualities of certain herbs and herbal potions, blood purifying pills and, best of all, an elixir of life, which amazingly guaranteed that just one spoonful a day was quite sufficient to work wonders. When passing through the front door, customers were confronted with solid, dark oak panelling, but on the left was a door that led into the temperance bar. To the right was a second door belonging to the herbalist shop. Both inner doors had loud warning bells. The temperance bar was large enough for a few small tables and chairs. On the far wall hung a well-used dartboard. Behind a high counter, tea- and coffee-making machines gleamed and steamed all day long. The advertised food, confectionery and cigarettes were all well displayed.

Now the herbalist shop was a wonder to behold. Everything about this section spoke of Victoriana. Behind a glass display counter — apart from a couple of framed diplomas — several shelves exhibited odd-shaped coloured bottles containing this and that, and all relating to the world of herbalism, and they in turn overlooked numerous small wooden drawers containing a variety of dried herbs, all appropriately identified.

Inside the glass counter was an array of coloured, differently sized cardboard boxes, bearing the names of certain medical aids: syringes, douches, nerve pills, poultices, salves, stimulants, and thick, washable French letters.

Between the two shops a short, narrow passageway led to living quarters at the rear. Dad was very friendly with Isaac Greenwood and usually on a Tuesday evening, when trade was slack, the two of them spent hours — talking remedies, they called it — behind Isaac's glass counter, and drinking Isaac's herbal tea. Dad, who was something of an amateur herbalist, would sometimes supply his friend with dried dandelion root and comfrey that he had collected on his many nature walks by the canal.

Aye, they got on well did Isaac and Dad, but it was quite obvious that Dad benefited most from this relationship. As Dad used to say, "Isaac knows a good many things tha knows, and talks a lot o' sense."

You see, apart from being a gentleman with a high, starched Victorian collar, bowler hat and pin-striped trousers, Isaac was also well read, and seemed to know something about everything. Dad was in awe of him, and pronounced on many occasions that "Education's a wondrous thing."

But one night, Dad's visits came to an abrupt end. Isaac died in his sleep.

On the day of the funeral, the undertaker — because of the intricate triple entrances — had to take his coffin out the back door, up an entry and along the street to a waiting hearse. Dad concluded that Isaac would have been turning in his coffin in utter disapproval. But he would still have been proud of the many congregational mourners, mostly poor folk, that lined the streets. Even the two burly wrestling brothers, Sid and Joe Mason, who had been regular customers, shed a tear as the hearse bearing Isaac's coffin, with his bowler hat sitting starkly amid the flowers, went slowly on its way.

Frances Greenwood never again opened her doors. Being childless, and having no one to share her grief, Frances became reclusive and the local community, thinking that this was the end of her and the business, went elsewhere.

For Frances, it was the end; but the business passed into the claw-like hands of a wizen, middle-aged bachelor, who wouldn't have looked out of place in a Humphrey Bogart picture.

With Isaac's name over-painted, a new name and title now appeared:

HORACE CARSHARPLE:
TWO SHOPS, ONE OWNER

And because he was new, this created curiosity and trade flourished.

However, Horace Carsharple knew nothing about herbalism and his ignorance in this delicate field of medicine soon became evident, as Minnie Sutch, one of his first customers, found out. Minnie was suffering from nervous exhaustion. Her husband, Jack, had died suddenly, leaving her with five children and an asthmatic mother-in-law who happened to live with them. Minnie, in desperation, decided to spend a little of what little money she had on a herbal cure. The cure she purchased from Horace Carsharple caused her to break out in boils, and not only that; when she mentioned to Carsharple that her husband had just passed away and she wanted something to cheer herself up, he suggested — with a leer — that she should get another man as soon as possible. When Minnie told Jack's mother, the old woman had a serious asthmatic attack, and she nearly joined her son,

Then it was the turn of Joe Mason, alias "Paraffin Joe" the wrestler. Joe had a bowel complaint which he blamed on the constant travelling he and his brother, Sid, "The Crusher" had to do to attend the many wrestling venues up and down the country. The brothers, inseparable as usual, called on Carsharple and introduced themselves. Horace, unimpressed, remarked that all wrestling, professional or otherwise, was just a game of pretend. The brothers, whose aggression in the ring was undisputed, ignored this offensive comment, and paid for a remedy that was guaranteed to solve Joe's problem. And it did! Joe had the trots for a week.

And because of his condition, he had to cancel a couple of well-paid wrestling bouts. Joe was not a happy man.

The word spread, and the realisation that Horace Carsharple's knowledge of herbs was indeed very dubious soon had people talking; that part of his business began to flounder. Dad, too, called it herbal quackery.

To compensate for this loss of trade, Carsharple turned his devious talents to gambling. And what better place for such a venture than his temperance bar? What authority would ever suspect that such a location would be used for the purpose of gambling?

Consequently, the place soon became a den for a few unscrupulous characters: Freddy Blake, a well-known layabout; Johnny Blackwood, a notorious black marketeer; and "Domino" Doran, who was reputed never to have lost a game of dominoes (for money, of course) in his life. And there were others, including a couple of rough, shady-looking characters, who watched over all proceedings with a beady eye.

And now, because of all this nefariousness, the owner became known as Horace "Cardsharp" because, in truth, that was what he was — a gambler and a cardsharp. Horace's sleight-of-hand trickery made him an all-time winner. This and his share of the takings from his shady cronies, not forgetting a couple of ladies of ill repute, gave Horace a decent income.

The end result of this iniquity was obvious. The poor — hoping for gain — became poorer, and Sid and Joe Mason's nephew, Harry, was one of those unfortunates who was lured into this uncertain world of chance.

Harry had always been a bit of a harum-scarum, and his uncles, Sid and Joe, had been approached by his mother to take him in hand; in other words, introduce him to the wrestling game. They did this gladly, but definitely on their terms, which were dedication to the sport, and to pay a weekly fee for his tuition and the upkeep of the gymnasium that had been built by existing and past members some years before.

A few months on and the signs were good. The lad, now steady and reliable, was enjoying the grappling game and coming on well. Anyhow, even the best of characters can, and do, succumb to the game of chance. And it was by chance that Harry fell victim to temptation. It happened one Saturday afternoon. Harry, who didn't drink, decided the temperance bar was an ideal stopping place for a glass of hot Vimto. Once inside, he was drawn into a game of poker, over which presided none other than Horace "Cardsharp" Carsharple. Harry lost all his money. Not one to give up easily, he returned to try his luck again ... and again ... and again ...

His absence from the gym alerted his uncles to something untoward and, when questioned, Harry told the truth. All his cash had been gambled away; he'd none left to pay his fees, or for owt else, for that matter.

In fact, he was still in debt to a tune of five pounds, and had been threatened by Carsharple's two surly, hard cases, for an immediate pay up, or else!

"Five pounds, did you say?" said Paraffin Joe.

"Aye, and the trouble is they've threatened to call at our house if I don't pay it quick."

"Don't worry about it," Sid the "Crusher" said. "Me and our Joe'll nip round and pay it off, won't we, Joe?"

"Aye, I reckon we will. I've never been one for debts."

And sure enough the visit was made. The five pounds were handed over to Carsharple.

Then Paraffin Joe, a gentleman to boot, asked him, in a quiet, gentle voice, wasn't it about time he acquired two new bodyguards?

"Not likely, not while I've got those two over there." He nodded in the direction of two rough-looking characters sat in a corner.

"Like I said," said Paraffin Joe, "I think it's about time you hired yourself two new bodyguards."

Carsharple was getting annoyed. "Hey, Jeff, Gerry, come and sort these two wallies out, will you?"

The ensuing battle was short, painful and bloody. Inside ten minutes, Carsharple's two henchmen were out for the count, and out on the pavement, while Carsharple took refuge behind the counter of his shop.

Hardly pausing for breath, Paraffin Joe reached over, grabbed his coat collar, and said, "Remember what you said about pretend? Well, you've just been a witness to the end of pretend, and to end it all, you'd better phone for an ambulance. Oh, and when you've done, pass the phone. I think the bobbies might have something to say about your end, don't you?"

And so it was. The police closed the place down and, in due time, like the property round and about, it was demolished.

126

It was the beginning of the end of an era. Horace Carsharple moved on, and so did his life. An out-of-town Boys' Club advertised for an assistant manager; against all odds, Horace, with no family connections, applied and got the job. And thus began a successful change of direction and character, that even Horace himself could never ever have imagined.

In his wake, the demolition men moved in; residents who had lived all their days side by side, suffering together the trials and tribulations of life, moved out. It seemed to some like they had gone to another planet and life would never be the same again. Churches, too — Protestant and Catholic — lost countless congregations; and were finally demolished.

And even the old Wigan Pier didn't escape those so-called wheels of progress, for that, too, in time to come, had to make way for the new.

"Goodbye, Wigan pier."

Wicksy

Peter Wicks

On my fourth birthday, I was presented with a beautifully made, yellow-painted pedal car. I remember that it had a horn, battery operated lights and a proper hand brake. I grew so attached to that car that I insisted upon having all my meals in it.

Brought up in and around Oxford, Peter Wicks brings his memoirs to life with a riot of colourful stories. From picnics with his parents via school days and bullies to spending summer holidays with his grandmother, Wicksy's tales are a charming look at a wartime childhood.

He also touches on the difficulties faced at the time, with air raid sirens, gas masks and wartime shortages, and the sad death of a childhood friend.

ISBN 978-0-7531-9502-4 (hb)
ISBN 978-0-7531-9503-1 (pb)

Hellfire and Herring

Christopher Rush

"You could smell God on the air in St Monans as surely as you could smell herring."

Hellfire and Herring is a vivid, powerful and moving account of Christopher Rush's upbringing in the 1940s and 1950s in St Monans, a small fishing village on the east coast of Scotland.

In an evocation of a way of life now vanished, Rush weaves stories from the fabric of family life, village characters, church and school. He writes of folklore and fishing, the eternal power of the sea and the cycle of the seasons. He also reflects on the relationship with his parents, and the inescapability of childhood influences far on into adult life.

ISBN 978-0-7531-9506-2 (hb)
ISBN 978-0-7531-9507-9 (pb)